BECOMING ENLIGHTENED

Also By Ron Scolastico, Ph.D.

THE MYSTERY OF THE CHRIST FORCE
A Personal Story of Enlightenment for Spiritual Seekers

DOORWAY TO THE SOUL
How to Have a Profound Spiritual Experience

REFLECTIONS
Inspired Wisdom on: Gods and Symbols; The Human Mind; Angels and Guides; Education; Healing Addictions; and, Healing the Hurt Child

HEALING THE HEART, HEALING THE BODY
A Spiritual Perspective on Emotional, Mental, and Physical Health

THE EARTH ADVENTURE
Your Soul's Journey Through Physical Reality

BECOMING ENLIGHTENED

Twelve Keys to Higher Consciousness

Ron Scolastico, Ph.D.

UNIVERSAL GUIDANCE PRESS

BECOMING ENLIGHTENED
Twelve Keys to Higher Consciousness

Copyright © 2008 by Ron Scolastico, Ph.D.

UNIVERSAL GUIDANCE PRESS
P.O. Box 6556
Woodland Hills, California 91365
www.ronscolastico.com
1-800-359-3771

All rights reserved, including the right of reproduction
in whole or in part in any form.

Manufactured in the United States of America

Library of Congress Cataloging-in-Publication Data
Scolastico, Ronald B. (Ronald Barry)
Becoming Enlightened/
Ron Scolastico

1. Spiritual life. 2. Experience (Religion) 3. Self-realization—
Religious aspects. I. Title.

ISBN 978-0-943-83317-0

It all depends on how we look at things, and not on how they are themselves.

Carl Jung

For Susan

Contents

PUBLISHER'S PREFACE	11
CHAPTER 1 *Beginning Your Journey of Discovery*	13
CHAPTER 2 *Exploring Your Spiritual Nature*	27
CHAPTER 3 *Preparing to Expand Your Consciousness*	43
CHAPTER 4 *The First Key, Expanding Your Vision of Yourself*	57
CHAPTER 5 *The Second Key, Expanding Your Vision of Your Soul*	71
CHAPTER 6 *The Third Key, Changing Limited Thought Patterns*	83
CHAPTER 7 *The Fourth Key, Mastering Your Expectations*	93
CHAPTER 8 *The Fifth Key, Engaging Your Life In the Present Moment*	103

CHAPTER 9
The Sixth Key, Practicing Expanding Your Awareness   111

CHAPTER 10
The Seventh Key, Opening Yourself Emotionally   125

CHAPTER 11
The Eighth Key, Transforming Your Negative Feelings   143

CHAPTER 12
The Ninth Key, Opening Your Intuition   165

CHAPTER 13
The Tenth Key, Opening to Your Soul   185

CHAPTER 14
The Eleventh Key, Creating an Ongoing Spiritual Focus   199

CHAPTER 15
The Twelfth Key, Exercising Patience   207

CHAPTER 16
Your Path of Enlightenment   215

Publisher's Preface

Becoming Enlightened presents material that was originally written by Dr. Ron Scolastico for an audio tape program entitled, "Twelve Keys to Higher Consciousness." In this book, Dr. Scolastico has greatly expanded the material, adding important new information for the reader.

Chapter 1

Beginning Your Journey of Discovery

---- ✺ ----

Welcome to a journey of self-discovery. In this book, I will show you how to open to a spiritual part of you that exists beyond your ordinary awareness. You will learn how to use twelve powerful keys to expand your awareness so that you can enter a higher state of consciousness to directly experience your limitless self, the part of you that is your *soul*. Learning to attain such experiences will enable you to create your own personal pathway to enlightenment.

As I guide you on your pathway, I will help you understand "enlightenment" in a clearer way than it is often understood. Some people have the idea that becoming enlightened is like being suddenly hit by a magical lightning bolt and becoming perfectly happy for life. They think that if they become enlightened they will no longer have any problems, immediately know all the mysteries of life, and have a constant awareness of the spiritual realities.

In this book I will help you gain a truer perspective so that you can understand that enlightenment is an ongoing *process*, rather than a single magical experience that transforms you forever. It is a process of training your awareness to expand beyond the limitations of ordinary human perceptions. By using the twelve keys to higher consciousness, you will create your personal enlightenment by a process of gradually introducing your human *self* into a direct experience of spiritual realities over a period of time through a daily silent practice.

Whether you are just beginning to investigate the mysteries of consciousness and the spiritual realities of life, or whether you are already on a spiritual quest and have spent some time exploring the inner world, in these chapters you will find what you need to discover the vastness of your total being—to experience who you *really* are. You will awaken to the extraordinary part of you that is your soul.

Perhaps you are at a point in your life where you are ready for more love, or deeper creativity, or more confidence in your own inner power to succeed in the world. Once you begin to use the twelve keys to higher consciousness you will open the way for those accomplishments. You will have the tools that you need to tap your full potential in the areas of your life that you want to master.

Together we will explore your spiritual nature, and

I will show you how to draw potent spiritual energies into your day to day experience. You will learn how to work with your thoughts and emotions to transform negative and painful feelings. I will show you ways to bring more love into your life. You will discover how to increase your intuition and break through the limits of ordinary awareness. And, you will learn a powerful step by step technique for journeying into the spiritual realm to discover for yourself the mysteries of your soul.

As a Spiritual Psychologist, one focus of my work through the years has been to try to bring the *soul* back into psychology. Years ago, psychology began as a study of the soul, but the focus later shifted to a study of the *mind*. Then came an emphasis on *behavior*. In recent years, there has been a strong focus on *the physiology of the brain*. Yet, many psychologists, researchers, and teachers are now recognizing the importance of the spiritual dimensions of life. Particularly in an international school of psychology that is called, *Transpersonal Psychology*, there has been a return to an interest in the soul and its place in our mental and emotional development.

Among the general public, there is now a real hunger for spiritual knowledge. This is apparent in the dramatic increase in books, magazines, movies, and television programs with a spiritual theme. It is clear that people have a growing desire for knowledge about the soul and the spiritual realities of life. And, many people want to learn how to directly experience their own soul.

After exploring the area of human consciousness

for more than 40 years, as well as working with thousands of individuals throughout the world, I have become convinced that everyone has an innate intuitive ability to experience their soul. By using the twelve keys to higher consciousness that you will be given in this book, you can learn to draw upon that ability within you so that you can become aware of your soul in a way that can open your path of personal enlightenment.

What you will read in these chapters is not just abstract theory. This knowledge comes from my own direct experience with the spiritual realities of life, and from the experiences of many of my students who have learned how to become aware of the spiritual realm. And, what is important for you to know is that all of those students are *normal people*.

Some people believe that they have to be unique or exceptional in order to expand their consciousness to have a profound spiritual experience. They believe that they need to be "psychic." That is not the case.

You have probably heard of people who say that they have been "psychic since childhood." Well, I have been *un*-physic since childhood. I am a normal person. I am not psychic. Yet, since 1978, I have had thousands of profound encounters with the spiritual realm. If I can make that kind of spiritual breakthrough, then you can do the same. And you can do it by using the twelve keys to higher consciousness.

After many years of entering the spiritual realms to connect with my soul, and seeing the results that my students have achieved through their spiritual growth,

I have come to believe that cultivating a deep spiritual connection is one of the most beneficial things that we can do for ourselves. It can open the door to everything that we desire in life.

In this book, I will show you how to achieve a deep spiritual experience. Then you will learn how to integrate that experience with a creative, satisfying personal growth process in your daily life.

When you consistently put together personal growth and spiritual experience, you will have everything that you need to live a more fulfilling life. You will be able to create more friendship and love with other people. You can experience stronger feelings of purpose and meaning in your life. You will have a fuller expression of your talents and abilities to succeed in the physical world. You will be able to work in a new way with your ordinary thoughts and feelings to unleash your full ability to be happy and successful in everyday life. You can use this book to create your own path of personal enlightenment and you will find that your day to day experiences will become much fuller, more satisfying, and quite exciting.

If you are not used to making a spiritual connection on a consistent basis, you might wonder how such an experience can benefit you. To show you what is possible, I will tell you about some of the beautiful changes that I have made in my own life. And, I have seen similar changes in the lives of many of my students all over the world.

One of the greatest benefits that I have gained from having spiritual experiences is a deep *emotional opening* within myself. Before I learned to connect with my soul, I was emotionally guarded. Because I had experienced so much emotional pain early on in my life, I did not want to have deep feelings. So, I essentially ignored my emotions and took a strictly intellectual approach to life. Essentially, I had a rather objective, somewhat impersonal attitude toward everything, including other people. The result was that my relationships with other people were usually shallow and unsatisfying. I was not able to fully open my heart to give and receive the love that I truly desired.

After learning what I will teach you in the following chapters, I gained the wisdom to clearly see the emotional blocks that I had unintentionally created through the years. I found the courage to begin to heal those blocks. As a result of that healing, I was able to discover a deep emotional sensitivity within myself that I began to share with other people. My relationships came alive with joy and greater love.

Connecting with the profound wisdom of my soul has also opened my *creativity*. It has made it possible for me to teach, write, and counsel other people in a deeper, more beneficial way. At times, the potency of the creativity has amazed me. For example, in writing my Doctoral dissertation, I was able to tap in to the creativity of my soul to write the four-hundred-page document from beginning to end in only five weeks. It is not unusual for someone to take five *years* to write their dissertation.

Many of my students who have learned to use the twelve keys to higher consciousness have made remarkable achievements in their lives. I have a student who is a well known Hollywood actress. At a time when she was struggling with her career, she learned to access the spiritual realm and connect with the deep creativity of her soul. The result was that she began to perform at a higher level in her film work. She got important new roles in major films, and eventually won the highest awards for her acting skills.

I believe that you, too, can use the twelve keys to access levels of your soul and experience wonderful openings in your life. Opening to your soul will not only bring you more creativity, joy, and love, but it will also put you in touch with a profound source of inner wisdom that can give you answers to questions that you have about life.

You have an intuitive "sixth-sense" inside you that can bring you valuable knowledge about life. By using the twelve keys to higher consciousness you can expand your awareness and access that powerful intuitive ability. Then, you can use your intuition to touch into knowledge that can dramatically enhance your day to day life.

My wife, Susan, has used the twelve keys for years, and has had many deep spiritual experiences. As a result, her intuition has become very strong. It has even saved us money.

We live in the Los Angeles area where there are a lot of earthquakes. But, for years, we never bothered to get earthquake insurance for our house. One day, Susan had a very strong intuitive feeling that we needed earthquake insurance. We followed her intuition, got the insurance, and two months later, a very powerful quake hit Los Angeles. We had hundreds of thousands of dollars worth of damage to our home. Thanks to Susan's intuition, it was all covered by the insurance.

Everybody is hungry for love. Our popular stories—the movies, television, books, magazines—are filled with the search for love. Learning to access spiritual levels can bring you the most satisfying love that you have ever experienced.

First of all, you will feel more love for *yourself*, because your connection with your soul will reveal to you how truly wonderful you are as a person. Then, with that increased sensitivity, you will feel kinder and more loving toward the people in your life, and that will open you to a deeper, fuller expression of love that you can share with everyone.

Most people have had the occasional feeling that there is no real purpose to their life. For some, this can become a constant, nagging sense of emptiness and despair. By learning to experience your soul, you can discover important purposes that your soul has for you in your life. Your feelings of lack of purpose can be healed.

For years, I felt that I had no purpose in my own life. I experimented with different occupations, but never felt right about any of them. After I learned to connect with my soul, I eventually discovered a deep desire to teach, and to counsel people. Since then I have had a very rewarding career as a teacher and spiritual counselor. I am convinced that these are important purposes in my life, and I believe that I would not have discovered them without the opening to my soul.

Connecting with your soul will put you in touch with a vast inner reservoir of talents and abilities that you have. You will gain the confidence to bring those abilities to their fullest expression in all areas of your life.

For example, you may have latent artistic abilities that you have never explored. As you begin to experience your soul, you could feel a deep stirring within yourself to draw upon those abilities to write, or paint, or express yourself through music. By tapping the inner strength from your soul, you could begin to feel so confident in those creative abilities that you would start to express your artistic talents in deeply satisfying ways.

❖

One of the greatest benefits of opening yourself spiritually is that it will help you discover deep connections that you have with other people. Such experiences can lead you to heal any feelings of loneliness and separation that you have had in the past, and can help you feel more deeply loved.

As you experience those deeper connections, you will be able to understand other people in a clearer way, and you will become more open and compassionate with them. That will make you more attractive to others, and you will naturally draw people to you in a more creative and loving way.

I once worked with an older woman named, Thelma, who was a nurse, and a widow. At the hospital where she worked, she was well known as a very stubborn and inflexible person. In fact, her co-workers called her "One-Way Thelma." Along with her stubbornness, she was extremely demanding and critical of everyone.

Because of her unpleasant and disagreeable personality, Thelma seemed to constantly alienate the people around her. As a result, she had no friends, and she was very lonely.

There was one nurse in particular, Christine, who actually hated Thelma. Thelma felt that hatred and grew to intensely dislike Christine. The animosity between them was so strong that they went so far as to change their shifts at the hospital so they would not have to work together.

After Thelma began to work with the twelve keys to higher consciousness her personality softened. She was able to see through her own defenses. Eventually, she was able to understand how she had created her loneliness by unintentionally driving people away. She wisely decided to make some changes in her behaviors.

One of the first things that she did was to get up the courage to go and talk to Christine, the nurse who hated her so much. Thelma apologized for her past behaviors and said that she wanted to get to know Christine. They met a few times over lunch and began to establish a friendship. Finally, they arranged to change their schedules at the hospital so that they could work together. Over time, they became good friends and established a deep relationship that helped Thelma heal her loneliness.

Another benefit of having a spiritual experience on a consistent basis is that you can gain the wisdom that you need to heal negative and painful feelings. Many people feel trapped in feelings of sadness, despair, fear, and other negative emotions. When you learn to tap in to the spiritual realm of your soul, you will be able to manage your emotions in a loving, creative way so that they no longer disrupt your life.

One of my students, Carl, is a physician whose brilliant teenage son was killed in an auto accident. After his son's death, Carl was extremely depressed for many months. He tried everything to heal his terrible feelings of loss. He saw a psychiatrist, threw himself into work, and even drank a lot. Nothing seemed to help.

Then, he started working with the twelve keys to expand his consciousness and open to his soul. That helped him to begin to transform his feelings of despair. Gradually, he had some deep experiences of the love and wisdom of his soul. Eventually, those experiences helped him to finally heal the terrible pain of the loss of his son. And, from time to time, he was even able to feel the comforting presence of the soul of his son. He later told me that his spiritual connection was the only thing that could have gotten him through such an ordeal.

I have worked with many people who were so overwhelmed by their negative feelings that they considered suicide to be the only way out of their pain. When they learned to connect with the love of their soul, they were able to transform their negative feelings and live joyful and fulfilling lives.

By connecting with your soul, you can also solve the great mystery of *death*. You can learn that *you* do not die when your physical body dies.

When I was in my early twenties, before I began my spiritual quest, I had a narrow, scientific, overly-intellectual view of life. I was convinced that my own personal existence would end at death. The idea of the soul, and an ongoing life beyond the physical world, seemed absurd to my rigid intellect. As a result of that limited and bleak attitude toward life, I developed a terrible fear of dying. I struggled with the fear, and I suffered from it for several years. At times, I got so discouraged about my hopeless view of life that I felt that there was really nothing to live for.

When I finally broke through to an awareness of my soul, and I learned to have ongoing spiritual experiences, I was able to lift myself out of that oppressive, hopeless vision to see through to a larger reality. My connection with my soul enabled me to directly experience the wonderful eternal aspect of me that will pass through the door of my physical death into the next stage of my journey. Those encounters with the larger realities of life helped me heal my fear of death.

❖

You can open the way for these kinds of benefits in your own life. The twelve keys to higher consciousness that you will learn in these chapters will give you the tools that you need to achieve wonderful, inspiring experiences for yourself. You will be able to create your own process of enlightenment that will lead to the fulfilling experiences that you desire in your life.

As you use these twelve keys, you will find that you will come alive in your career, your creative endeavors, and your relationships with other people. You will feel a vibrant and exciting newness in everything that you do, as if you have stepped into a thrilling new world of beauty and magnificence. You will feel such deep purpose and meaning in your life that each moment can seem to be part of an important *quest* that you have been on all your life. Your work with the twelve keys will enable you to use your full talents and abilities to create great joy for yourself, and to more deeply appreciate and love the people in your life.

Chapter 2

Exploring Your Spiritual Nature

---- ❋ ----

Now that you know some of the benefits of making a connection with the spiritual realm, in order to begin your preparation for using the twelve keys to higher consciousness to move toward having your own spiritual experience, we will look more closely at the nature of spiritual experiences, and of the soul. In this chapter I give you some basic definitions of the terms, "spiritual experience," and "soul," that you can use as a starting point for your own process of enlightenment.

Each person will have their own unique experience of the spiritual realm. For those who might be confused about how a spiritual experience is different from an ordinary experience, and to give you a fuller sense of what a spiritual experience can be like, I will briefly summarize some experiences that were important aspects of my own spiritual quest. These are described in detail my book, *The Mystery of The Christ Force: A Personal Story of Enlightenment for Spiritual Seekers.*

I had my first spiritual experience when I was eight years old. But, I did not know what it was, and it deeply frightened me.

I was lying on my bed one afternoon, reading a book. All of a sudden, without any warning, I started to feel myself expanding beyond my body. I was just lying there feeling myself growing larger and larger. Pretty soon, I felt like I was filling up my whole room.

I was terrified. I had no idea what was going on. I struggled to move, but my body did not respond. For a minute, I thought I might be dying. Finally, I inwardly shook myself and my body began to move. I jumped up and ran out of my room.

That strange event was so traumatic that I immediately blocked it out of my mind. The next day I had no memory of what had happened.

❖

More than thirty years later, my forgotten childhood experience would play a large part in my spiritual awakening. It was the late seventies and I had just completed my doctoral program in Psychology and Human Communication Studies. I was working with a spiritual teacher who was helping me expand my awareness. Under her patient guidance, I was able to release my fear of unusual states of consciousness.

At one point in our work together, my teacher told me that I had the ability to enter a deep state of consciousness and draw on a source of universal wisdom to do spiritual counseling for people. Although I trusted her opinion, I was very skeptical about my ability to tap in to such a source. So, I devised a method to test myself.

Each day, I sat in silence, entered a meditative state, and spoke words aloud. I tape recorded what I said so that I could analyze it later.

At first, what came out in those daily sessions seemed to be nothing more than my own thoughts. Then, I started to receive information about some of my friends. I was not really confident that the information was accurate, so I decided to give the tapes to my friends to get their reactions. Surprisingly, they told me that the information was very helpful and inspiring. Some even asked me to do another tape for them.

After several months of making these tapes alone, a good friend talked me into doing an "in person" session for her while she was in the room. I told her about my skepticism and cautioned her to be flexible about what I said from my deep state, and to view it as an experiment.

I began her session in my usual way. First, I closed my eyes, said a brief affirmation, then released into my meditative state. After I reached that state, I began to speak words in the same way that I had done in my recorded sessions alone.

After speaking to her from my meditative state for about ten minutes, all of a sudden, I began to feel myself expanding. I started to feel like I was going beyond my body, growing larger and larger. Soon, I felt like I was filling up the whole room. And, along with the sense of expansion, I had a very profound feeling of love.

This had never happened in the sessions that I had done alone. I thought: "This is amazing. What an incredible experience."

When the expansion began, I had stopped talking from the meditative state. I just sat there in silence, awed by the experience that I was having.

Finally, my voice picked up again and started talking to my friend. It told her that I had been lifted out of my body and had been expanded so that I could more deeply connect with the universal source of wisdom. Then, my voice said: *"This experience was implanted in him when he was eight years old so it could be returned at this time so that he would believe."* Meaning, so that I would believe in my ability to do spiritual counseling from a deep state of consciousness.

Since I had totally forgotten that childhood experience, when I heard this statement I was astounded. I instantly recalled the event that had been so frightening when I was eight, and I knew that whatever had caused me to leave my body as a child was now helping me develop my ability to reach higher levels of consciousness. Later, I came to understand that it was my soul guiding me to open myself so that I could teach and help people.

That experience of leaving my body in the session with my friend many years ago opened the way for me to have spiritual experiences suited to my own personality. By practicing the twelve keys to higher consciousness, you can learn to have profound spiritual experiences in your own unique way that will be most meaningful for you.

❖

At this point, I will clarify what a "spiritual experience" actually is. First of all, it can be thought of as *an inner event* that lifts us beyond the ordinary human world into a realm of expanded awareness and heightened experiences. It is a breakthrough to a larger reality than the one we normally experience in our day to day lives in the physical world. Unlike our life in the physical world that can seem negative and threatening at times, this larger reality is one that is filled with perfect goodness, beauty, and love.

A spiritual experience can differ from person to person. However, through the years I have discovered certain similarities in the spiritual experiences of different people throughout the world. They include:

1. Feelings of bliss and ecstasy.
2. Experiences of profound love for all beings.
3. A deep sense of the holiness of life.
4. A vast feeling of universal oneness and harmony with all existence.
5. An encounter with the perfection of the creative source of all life.

On a more subtle level, a certain kind of "spiritual" experience can come as a deep and moving feeling of being connected with the beauty of nature, powerful inspiration that someone feels from a work of art, or the uplifting experience that comes from loving a child. It is possible to have a form of spiritual experience in moments ranging from the mundane to the cosmic.

One of the most dramatic and awe inspiring spiritual experiences is a profound feeling of the presence of what many people understand as *God*. Such an experience can be attained by people who follow a religion, as well as by those who have their own individual spiritual path apart from organized religion.

❖

What I have personally experienced in my more dramatic breakthroughs to spiritual realities is similar to the beautiful descriptions given by people who have had *near-death* experiences. In the near-death encounter, the person's physical body is considered to be clinically dead, but the consciousness of the person journeys into a reality that lies beyond ordinary human awareness.

In my own deep encounters with the spiritual reality, I move through several stages that are similar to the stages that many near-death experiencers have described.

First, I am aware of a sense of inner movement, away from my physical body. I feel as if I am moving out of the physical reality into a new, non-physical world. There are no limits in this wonderful inner world, and I can move about freely, unrestrained by the heaviness of physical reality. Similarly, in the near-death experience, many people report a releasing movement. They feel that they are moving along a corridor or pathway, or through a tunnel. Then they break out into a vast new limitless world where they feel amazingly free and unrestricted.

Next, I come into a brilliant new reality that is filled with radiant love. This love seems to emanate brightly from an extremely powerful source. Many people who have had near-death encounters tell of experiencing a brilliant source of love, or a marvelous light that they feel is projecting love toward them.

Then, I sense a most profound presence of kindness, compassion, and goodness. I feel as if some extraordinarily nurturing power is embracing me and bringing me an incredible sense of well-being. This is similar to what many near-death reports describe as an encounter with exalted spiritual beings, or the spiritual presence of loved ones.

There follows for me a penetration into a vast source of knowledge and wisdom that seems to be unlimited in its scope. This source seems to have answers to all of life's questions. In the near-death experience, many people feel that are being taught deep truths about all of existence. They come away with a penetrating new understanding of life.

During my spiritual experiences, I have a direct perception of the eternal nature of our existence. It is perfectly clear to me that we only temporarily live in physical bodies, and that our true existence is in the spiritual realm. I feel a remarkable sense of perfection, and it is evident that such perfection resides deep within every human being.

In all of my spiritual experiences, I have become aware of what many people have discovered in their own spiritual encounters: *There is an extraordinary, unending spiritual force of love that continually sustains our human selves.* Awakening to that love is the most fulfilling experience that I have ever known.

You may not immediately have such a dramatic spiritual experience when you first begin your inner work. Yet, when you are using the twelve keys to expand your consciousness, even your more subtle preliminary openings can be inspiring and satisfying. Then, as you become more adept at working with the keys, you can open the way for a deeper spiritual experience. That will set you off on your pathway of enlightenment.

I will be using the term, *soul*, a lot in this book. So, before we go any further, I want to give you a picture of the soul that you can use as a focal point in your movement toward your own spiritual experience. This will help you understand the relationship between your human self and your soul.

The first step in becoming consciously aware of your soul is to consistently focus on meaningful *concepts* about your soul. Your concepts can serve as a starting point for your inner journey to a discovery of the actual existence of your soul in the spiritual realm.

However, it is important to remember that concepts are simply human-created explanations. They are human *ideas* about the nature of reality. In working with the twelve keys to higher consciousness you can begin with the concept of the soul that I will suggest for you, then that can be used as a springboard into a direct experience of the reality of your soul. Through such experiences you will discover for yourself the true nature of your soul in a way that goes beyond concepts.

As a teacher, I have had to spend a lot of time thinking about the soul, so I have explored many concepts. But, you want to *experience* your soul, not simply intellectualize about it. The difference between intellectualizing about your soul and experiencing it is similar to the difference between writing a thesis on love, and actually being in love. Your work with the twelve keys can take you beyond conceptualizing to a profound and satisfying experience of your soul.

As you begin to work with the concept of the soul that I will give you, keep in mind that you do not need to *prove* anything about the soul. After all of my years of study and inner exploration, first in studying concepts about the soul, and then later directly experiencing my own soul, it has become clear to me that we cannot objectively prove the existence of the soul. We cannot prove the truth of the soul, nor can we say in precise words what the soul is like. That is because the soul is not a physical manifestation in the outer world that can be measured, tested, and objectively verified. The soul is perceived within the inner subjective reality of each individual.

Some concepts are rooted in the reality of the soul, while others are not. I have worked with many people who had the idea that their soul has the same limitations that we as humans have. There are books written that describe the soul as needing to be "cared for," and "educated," and "trained" in order to evolve. The soul is seen as an imperfect entity that needs to be improved in order to advance to some higher level of existence. I find such ideas very uninspiring. If my soul is as flawed as I am, I do not want to turn to my soul for wisdom and guidance.

From thousands of personal experiences with the

spiritual realm, and from vast knowledge that has been given in many spiritual readings that I have done through the years, I have come to believe that the concept that I will now share with you presents a relatively clear picture of the reality of your soul. It is a powerful vision of the soul that has deeply enriched my own life, and has inspired many of my students in their process of moving toward a direct experience of their own soul. What is important for you is not to try to prove that this concept is the truth about the soul, but to test this concept in your inner experience to see if it inspires you on your path of enlightenment.

To begin to explore the various levels of this concept of the soul, you can start with this thought:

> **Your soul is the perfect part of you that is eternal. Your soul existed before your birth into this lifetime, and your soul will continue to exist after your physical death.**

Next, understand that your soul has its existence and expresses in a dimension of reality that lies *beyond time and space*. However, the "energies" of your soul are woven into your physical existence while you are alive as a human on earth. Your soul is your wonderful, perfect, totally loving, true being that resides in the spiritual realm, but it also shares your human life with you.

Then, another aspect of your soul to place into your thoughts is this: *Your soul constantly interacts with all other souls in the spiritual realm, and with the creative forces of life that many people think of as God.*

Now, here is a very important point for you to understand. At first, some of my students have had difficulty imagining how this might be, so think deeply about this: *You are your soul right now, in this moment.* While you are temporarily experiencing yourself as a human being inside your physical body within time and space, you are also *simultaneously* existing as your soul in a perfect, non-physical, spiritual realm beyond time and space.

To help envision how this might be, imagine that in this moment you are your soul existing before your birth in this lifetime. As a soul, you are aware of other souls. You are aware of the magnificent beauty of the spiritual realm. You are participating in the mighty and unlimited creative forces of life in the non-physical world.

Now, imagine that *you-as-a-soul* decide to express yourself as a human being in the physical world on earth. You bring this about by drawing upon the cosmic creative forces of life that many people call, God, and, as a co-creator with God, *you-as-a-soul* initiate an extraordinary process of unfoldment that will lead to the manifestation of the human being that is you right now.

First, drawing upon the divine energies of creation, *you-as-a-soul* create *a human personality structure of energies*. Your personality structure is what you will come to experience as your human *self*. It is the part of you that you are now familiar with as your inner conscious life.

You-as-a-soul then project what you might call a

single "ray" of your own divine soul consciousness into this human personality structure of energies. This divine ray of soul consciousness gives your personality structure the capacity *to be aware of itself.* You are given the divine gift of *self-awareness.* This self-awareness enables your personality structure to subjectively experience itself as one individual set apart from all others. It enables you to feel: "I am *me.*"

Now, imagine that it is time for your present physical body to be born on earth. As the birth of your body occurs, your soul brings forth the human personality structure of energies it has created, and, so to speak, "projects" that personality structure into your newborn infant body.

As you grow as a child, your personality structure with its self-awareness is experienced as *you.* You have the ongoing experience of your personality structure as being your personal thoughts, feelings, beliefs, memories, desires, likes, dislikes, physical sensations, and so forth. As *you-as-a-human-being* have that subjective experience throughout your lifetime, it is "shared" by *you-as-a-soul.*

However, your soul gives your personality structure a limited conscious awareness so that you can remain focused on physical reality. That enables you to live your human life with full intensity, but it blocks your human awareness of your true existence as an eternal soul. If your human self had a full conscious awareness of your soul's existence, the remarkable radiance and majesty of your soul's divine experience would so overshadow your human experience that you would find it difficult to sustain an interest in your human life.

Some people who have had extremely deep spiritual experiences, particularly dramatic near-death encounters, have become so fully aware of the magnificence of their soul existence that they do not want to return to their ordinary human life. In comparison to the splendor of their soul existence, they find the physical world to be pale and without meaning. So, to help you maintain a meaningful focus on your human life, your soul has brought down a temporary "veil" over your human consciousness so that you will not be overwhelmed by a full awareness of your eternal existence as a soul.

Yet, even though your conscious awareness of your soul is intentionally veiled in order to allow you to fully appreciate and enjoy your human experience on earth, you can choose to expand your awareness to gain a certain experience of your soul that can deeply inspire you without overshadowing your human life.

It is important to realize that your human personality self structure is a temporary vehicle that you use to live your life inside your physical body. When your physical body dies, that personality self structure will be released from your body and it will gradually be taken up into your soul.

From my own personal experiences, and from my research, I have come to believe that, immediately after your death, you will experience yourself still within your personality self structure, and you will feel something like this: "I have just left my physical body behind and I am still *myself.* I am now floating in a world that is not physical." At that point, you will experience yourself as being similar to a human being. You will feel like you are an individual self in your personality structure.

While you are in that limited, but brief, human personality structure stage after your death, you will self-create your subjective experience. You will create that experience according to the strong, primary beliefs that you consistently held in your human life before your death.

For example, in your human life, if you strongly believed in "hell," then, after your death, you might possibly create a subjective experience of suffering in hell. If you believed that there is a God, then after your death you would self-create a subjective experience of God. That perception of God would be framed in your human concepts and beliefs about God. If you believed in Jesus as your spiritual focus, you would experience his presence. A belief in Buddha would result in an experience of Buddha.

This period of self-creating from within the personality self structure after death will be very brief. It might not even occur for those who, during their human life on earth, opened their hearts, studied diligently, and tried to know the largest truth about life that they could know. Such individuals would begin to self-create experiences that would be similar to the *real* qualities of their true eternal existence. Those would be experiences of perfect harmony, beauty, and love.

❖

Eventually, after your death, you will put aside all self-created subjective experiences of your personality self structure. You will peel away all human illusions. Then, as a self-contained personality self structure, you will begin to drift out of your lingering human perspective toward the eternal reality of your soul.

At first, you will see your soul quite clearly as a discreet, separate, eternal being of extraordinary majesty. Then, gradually, as you move closer to your soul, your personality self structure will begin to loosen and expand. Your awareness inside your personality structure will grow. It will become larger and larger as you come closer to your soul. When you finally come to your soul, your personality self structure awareness will expand quite dramatically. Then, *your personality self structure awareness will begin to merge with your soul awareness.*

At that point, you will feel within yourself: "I *am* the eternal soul. *I-as-an-eternal-soul* have projected this personality self structure into that human body that has died. Now, *I-as-an-eternal-soul* lovingly welcome this personality self structure back into my eternal being."

Then, *you-as-a-soul* will be enriched and expanded by the human experiences that your personality self brings to you from its life on earth.

While you are working with the twelve keys to higher consciousness to achieve an experience of your soul, in order to remember that *you are your soul*, it can be helpful to simply think of your soul as a very real and wonderful experiential "place" inside you. When you go to that place, you will feel like you have come home.

You can also think of your soul as a vast reservoir of wisdom, courage, strength, creativity, comfort, talents, abilities, and even wise answers to your questions about your life. That reservoir exists inside your personality self structure, and you can learn to tap in to it to draw upon those beneficial gifts from your soul.

Your soul is your personal connection to the larger spiritual realities of life. It is your personal doorway to the eternal realm.

These are some concepts that you can use as a foundation for your work with the twelve keys to higher consciousness. As you do that inner work, this vision of your soul can guide you. It will help you move toward a direct experience of your own soul.

When you actually experience the reality of your soul, you will transcend all human thoughts and concepts. You will have a new kind of inner knowing about yourself as a human personality self, and as an eternal being. Then, you will not need to be limited to intellectual ideas and concepts. You will have your own undeniable experience of your soul existing in the spiritual realm. That experience will then be the foundation upon which your build your pathway of enlightenment.

Chapter 3

Preparing to Expand Your Consciousness

---------※---------

As you set out to expand your consciousness to gain an awareness of your soul, and to create your own pathway of enlightenment, you can begin with the understanding that woven into the very fabric of the physical world is an extraordinary non-physical spiritual reality. Your soul and other souls exist in that spiritual reality. The energies of those souls intermingle with the physical world. By using the twelve keys to higher consciousness, you can learn to draw upon those energies in a way that will enable you to gain an awareness of the spiritual reality and directly experience your soul.

To experience the spiritual reality of your soul, you will need to use a different kind of awareness than what you normally use to perceive the physical reality of your life on earth. To experience the physical world, you use your ordinary awareness. To experience the spiritual realm, you will learn to use a *second* awareness that will take you beyond the physical world.

You can compare your human awareness to a television receiver that has two channels. When you are tuned in to the first channel, you cannot receive the second one. To receive the second channel you need to switch channels on your receiver.

For purposes of the inner work that you will do to expand your consciousness, you can consider that you have two distinct and separate channels in your human awareness. Think of the first channel as your *ordinary awareness* through which you are conscious of your normal thoughts, feelings, and other inner experiences, as well as your perceptions of the outer physical world.

The second channel of your awareness is what I call your *Extraordinary Awareness*. When you are tuned in to that channel you can directly perceive the non-physical spiritual realm.

Many people are not even aware that they have the second channel of Extraordinary Awareness. So, by default, they are always tuned in to their first channel of ordinary awareness. Their attention is constantly focused on the physical world, and they are not aware that anything else exists. That allows them to create a great deal of intensity in their physical life, but it also limits their discovery of the majesty, beauty, and love of their soul existence.

Although your Extraordinary Awareness is usually

obscured by the activity of your ordinary awareness as you live your daily life in the physical world, you can learn to shift to your second channel of higher awareness. When you do that, you can transcend any limits that you may experience in ordinary awareness. Using your Extraordinary Awareness, you can perceive the spiritual realm as it intermingles with physical reality.

As I mentioned earlier, *you-as-a-soul* intended for *you-as-a-human* to focus primarily on your human life in the physical world. That focus enables you to create a personal, experiential intensity that allows you to fully live your human existence. However, at the same time, your soul has given you an inner desire to expand your awareness so that you will not completely limit yourself to your life in physical reality. But, your soul does not demand that you act on that desire. It is up to you to decide if you want to expand your awareness or not.

Yet, your soul has placed into your personality self structure a powerful curiosity, and a yearning to know more about all aspects of life. If you follow that impulse and discover your second channel of Extraordinary Awareness, then you can add an experience of spiritual realities to your human life. That will make your life richer, more joyful, and more filled with love.

In order not to interfere with your free will, the soul impulse that urges you to discover the spiritual reality acts beneath your conscious awareness. You can choose to ignore that impulse and it will remain dormant throughout your life. Or, you can choose to expand your consciousness and bring that impulse from your soul into your conscious awareness. That will stimulate a desire to open to a larger reality, to discover your channel of Extraordinary Awareness through which you can gain a direct experience of your soul and the spiritual realities.

As you get ready to open to an awareness of your soul, it is very important to know that you will be working with *the subjective reality that occurs within your inner life*. Your awareness of the spiritual forces of your soul will be subjective. You will not expect to see your soul as a physical form in the outer, objective world. You will perceive your soul in your inner experience.

This means that in your first channel of ordinary awareness, the link to your second channel of Extraordinary Awareness is *your subjective reality*—your inner life of thinking, feeling, imagining, and intuitive sensing. By making certain adjustments in your subjective reality that you will learn in these chapters, you can shift to your second channel of Extraordinary Awareness. Through that higher awareness you can travel the inner pathway of enlightenment that leads to the spiritual reality of your soul.

Your inner life of spiritual awakening is quite different from your outer life of achievement in the physical world. The outer world is a place of *action*. A certain type of action is important in your inner life, but the kind of inner "actions" that you will take to open your awareness to your soul will be quite different from the actions that you take in the outer world.

When you act to accomplish something in the outer world, expressions of *will, force,* and *determina-*

tion are very important. On the other hand, the inner actions that you will take to gain a conscious awareness of your soul will be very *subtle, gentle, receptive,* and essentially *passive.* Because they are so subtle, at times they can seem vague, tenuous, and even "invisible."

In taking those subtle inner actions, you will not be able to immediately manipulate things like you can in the physical world. When you sit in silence to shift to your Extraordinary Awareness to tune in to your soul, you cannot manipulate your consciousness like you can physical objects in the outer world.

Expanding your consciousness to become aware of your soul requires gentle, receptive adjustments patiently carried out over a period of time. Through that process, you will learn how to shift to your second channel of Extraordinary Awareness to become conscious of your soul.

So, keep in mind that in the outer world you can take actions *rapidly* and succeed by *manipulating*. In the inner world, as you work to create an awareness of your soul, your inner actions will be taken *gradually*, and you will succeed by *receiving*.

As you open to an awareness of your soul in your inner life, you will be engaging a *non*-physical reality. When you engage a non-physical reality, you will draw upon your qualities of *emotional sensitivity, creativity, intuition, receptivity,* and *trust* in order to open your second channel of Extraordinary Awareness. This is quite different from the qualities needed for success in the outer world. In the physical world where there are tangible factors to be mastered, you often need boldness, strength, forcefulness, and determination, and you only need to rely upon your first channel of ordinary awareness.

In later chapters, you will learn a special inner process that I have developed through the years that will help you use your more sensitive qualities to experience your soul. I call that process an *attunement* because it involves *tuning in* to the energy of your soul and the spiritual realm. You will learn to open your Extraordinary Awareness to make an attunement to your soul as part of your implementation of the twelve keys to higher consciousness.

As you use the attunement process, it will be important to be aware that when you tap in to your soul, the experience will take you beyond words and ideas. Words and ideas are part of the physical world. The communication that goes on between your soul and your human self is *non*-physical. It is carried out through non-physical energies.

You cannot perceive those energies through your physical senses. You cannot hear them, see them, touch them, smell them, or taste them. However, you can *feel* them. And, it is through your deep intuitive feelings that you will become aware of your soul's communication to your human self.

When you first learn to experience the energies of your soul that communicate to you through your feelings, you may not know what the feelings mean. You may not know what your soul is trying to communicate to you. So, you will need to learn a new language. It is a language of feelings, not words.

I will use an image here to illustrate this. Imagine that the communications of your soul are like the growl of a bear. When you hear the bear growling, you know that it is a communication from the bear, but, you cannot understand it. You do not know what the growling means. Maybe it is a warning, or maybe it is calling to another bear. The bear's language of growling is of an entirely different nature than the reality created by the words of human language.

If you want to understand the communication of the bear, you do not wait for the bear to use *your* language of human words. That is not likely to happen. You will need to learn the language of growling that the bear uses to communicate. In the same way, you will not wait for your soul to speak to you in human words. You will learn the language of *feelings* that your soul uses to communicate with you.

To learn the feelings language of your soul, you will need to step out of your human experience and enter the reality of your soul. You can do that by making a magical transformation through the use of your *imagination*.

Many people underestimate the importance of imagination. They think that what they imagine is simply fantasy. Since *reality* is what is important, then imagination must be insignificant because it is not reality. What they do not realize is that imagination is an inner power that can be used to initiate a profound expansion of consciousness.

You can create an imagination of your soul's reality that may at first seem like it is not real. Yet, that imagination can set into motion an opening of your intuitive ability that can lead you from simply imagining your soul's reality to actually perceiving it with your inner sensing.

Starting off with an imagination "primes the pump" of consciousness, so to speak. It gets your inner sensing flowing. Then, the momentum created by your imagining pushes your awareness to expand until you actually begin to perceive your soul's reality. What begins as a human imagination leads to a direct perception of spiritual reality.

You can use your imagination to begin to learn your soul's language of feelings. A very powerful way to do this is to imagine a *form* for the non-physical energies that your soul uses to communicate with your human self. Such an imagining can be combined with the attunement method that you will learn later.

A form that I find effective to use for the non-physical energies of the soul's language is *light*. I imagine the energies of my soul communicating with me in the form of a beautiful, brilliant light flowing all around me.

When you are opening yourself to your soul, even though you do not see your soul in a physical form, you can create a strong inner opening by imagining that you are actually perceiving the communications of your soul as energies of light. You can imagine that brilliant, beautiful light surrounding and embracing you. That imagining can create a jumping off point to begin to move toward experiencing the reality of your soul, including your soul's language of feelings.

After you imagine the beautiful light all around you, then you can begin to imagine that the light is conveying a special meaning to you. Just as the growl of the bear had meaning, this light from your soul has meaning. The problem is that the light is like the bear's growl. You do not know what the meaning is.

As you imagine the light all around you as a language of feelings that your soul is speaking, you can say to yourself: "I desire to understand what my soul is communicating to me with these non-physical energies that I am perceiving as light." To accomplish that, you will use the power of your imagination to *become* the light. That will enable you to enter the reality of your soul.

If you only look at the light, it is simply bright energy that you are perceiving from outside the light. It is interesting, and it might even inspire you, but you have no idea what it means. You do not know what it is communicating to you. You can try to interpret it through your own thoughts, but, that is not always a clear perception of what your soul is actually communicating to you. To truly understand the communication from your soul, you will need to *enter* the light.

Again, you will summon up the power of your imagination. You can begin by saying to yourself: "To know what my soul is communicating to me, I will now become this light from my soul."

Yet, these words are just the beginning. You will not become the light from your soul by just thinking words. Words are creations used for speaking a *human* language. You will need creations that are used in the language of your soul.

Knowing that the language of your soul is feelings, then, when you begin to enter the energy of light that is your soul's communication, you will not use words to think about the light. You will become the light by using your feelings.

Using your imagination and your feelings, you will experience yourself entering the beautiful light coming from your soul. You will leave behind all thoughts and words. You will use the power of your imagination to enter fully into the light. Then, you will begin to notice what it feels like inside the magnificent light that is coming from your soul.

Imagine that inside this light you feel a profound *comfort*. Then, you will enter those feelings of comfort and you will allow yourself to be deeply penetrated by them. You will allow yourself to be completely saturated with the feelings of comfort.

Then, at that point, you can use your mind to think: "Since I am feeling profound comfort inside this light of communication from my soul, perhaps my soul is saying to me in its language of feelings, 'I am here with you, and I am comforting you, and loving you.'"

In this soul communication, there are no words involved, except the words that you think in your mind after you experience the profound feelings of comfort. The words are human, and they allow you to understand the experience. But, the energy of profound comfort from your soul is *divine*.

Your soul is using divine spiritual energies to

comfort you and to communicate to you: "I am here and I am loving you." You have translated the spiritual energies into words, but you have done it directly from the profound *feelings* of comfort that you perceived inside the light energy from your soul. If you had not felt the feelings of profound comfort, you could have imagined *any* words about the light.

For example, if you had simply seen the light from outside of it, you could have said: "The light means that my soul is saying to me, 'Go forth and strike a match.'" Without the feelings to guide you, you could imagine anything about the light. Since your soul is communicating in its feeling language and not in words, if you have no feelings connecting you to the truth of your soul's communication, then any words that you might imagine about that communication can be confused.

Now, here is a very important point: If you learn to enter the feelings of your soul's communication to you, then *the words that the feelings stimulate in your mind can be a clear representation in human language of the underlying **truth** of your soul's communication that is coming to you in non-physical energy forms.*

When you are using your imagination in the way that I have described, at first, you may not feel that you are actually perceiving a real communication from your soul. Yet, if you keep working in this way, what at first seems to be only imagination will gradually begin to take on a life of its own. Your soul will help you and guide you to move from your self-initiated imagination to a very real experience of your soul. You will feel the deepening of the experience, and you will eventually realize that you are not simply imagining your soul, but you are truly beginning to inwardly perceive the reality of your soul.

You will begin by using your imagination to prime the pump of consciousness to stimulate your Extraordinary Awareness, but then, you will learn how to put your own *will* aside, and your inner experience can then be guided by your soul. You will put aside your human choosing about what to experience, and you will become aligned with a deep, intuitive feeling of what the communicating energies from your soul desire to express to you. Eventually, you will be able to directly experience the truth that is contained in the energies of the language of feelings being spoken by your soul.

There is a very powerful process that takes place as you learn to put aside your will in your inner exploration. As you cease to consciously choose what occurs, *your inner experience can be created by your soul.* Your soul will trigger the experiences that will be most important in your growth and unfoldment in human life. You will feel a profound sense of being guided and taught in ways that will lead to the accomplishment of your true purposes in life.

When you open your heart to the magnificence of your soul in this way, you will learn to receive wisdom and truth from the divine realm of your soul. At first, you might experience that as feelings of comfort, love, and wonderful goodness. Then, in time, during your attunement to your soul, you may experience inspiring thoughts that spontaneously appear in your mind, not consciously chosen by you.

As this happens, it is not wise to immediately say: "These thoughts are a communication from my soul." But, you could consider that perhaps the inspired thoughts are a *translation* of the communication from your soul. That translation is created by your human self. The accuracy of the translation will be determined by the quality of your human personality.

If you are essentially honest, sensitive, intelligent, and not overly distorted by negative thoughts and emotions, then that may be a translation of truth into human words. To make certain of that, you can work with the inspired thoughts and use your human intelligence to test them in your day-to-day life.

You have an innate wisdom within you. If you take time each day to attune to your soul, and if you are honest and loving in your daily life, then, eventually, you will be able to use your Extraordinary Awareness more and more, and that can bring profound knowledge and guidance from your soul into your human personality self. You will find your own unique way to understand and experience your soul. And that will lead to the blossoming of your full potential in all areas of your life. It will become the enlightenment that you have been seeking on your spiritual pathway.

Chapter 4

The First Key: Expanding Your Vision of Yourself

---- ✵ ----

Now that you have some basic concepts about your soul, you can begin to work with the first key to higher consciousness, which is: *Expanding your vision of yourself as a person.* In this chapter I will help you begin to break through any limited beliefs that you might have about yourself. This is important because your limited beliefs can create inner blockages that will stand in the way of opening your second channel of Extraordinary Awareness.

As you set out on your path of enlightenment to gain a conscious awareness of the magnificence of your soul and the spiritual realm, it will be very important to make certain that the vision that you have of yourself as a person is *large* enough. To move toward a deep experience of your soul, you will need to expand your limited beliefs about who you are as a person. You will need to create powerful positive beliefs about yourself in order to begin the process of inner opening that will eventually lead you to larger truths about who you really are.

If you see yourself as small and unworthy, you can create a feeling that your limited human self is very different from the vast goodness of your soul. With such beliefs about yourself, you might create an expectation that it may take years of work to improve yourself before you are good enough to deserve being loved by your soul.

Or, if you underestimate yourself and your abilities, you will have difficulty believing that you are sensitive enough and talented enough to be able to make an expansion of your consciousness to actually become aware of your soul. Such limited beliefs about yourself can lead you to feel that there are many obstacles on your path of enlightenment.

On the other hand, if you can feel the true goodness of yourself as a human being, then you will be able to believe that your personality self shares some of the same beautiful and wonderful qualities as your soul. You will be able to believe that there is no great difference between you and your soul, which will make it easier, as you move along in the process of enlightenment, to awaken to the truth that there is no *distance* between you and your soul.

The First Key: Expanding Your Vision of Yourself 59

You will eventually come to know that your soul is not limited by time and space. You will be able to experience that your soul *is with you at all times*. Then, you will realize that it will not be so difficult to bring your human awareness into alignment with your soul. Your goal of personal enlightenment will seem much more attainable.

If your beliefs about yourself cause you to feel that you are small and limited, then you will find it difficult to love your personality self. If you cannot love yourself, then you will feel that you are not a worthy person. That feeling can create tight, negative emotional patterns inside you that can limit you when you try to expand your consciousness to become aware of your soul.

The most potent feelings to inwardly create in order to release and expand your consciousness are feelings of openness and love. If you begin by creating strong feelings of love for yourself, then the stage is set for creating the general feelings of expansiveness and love that are needed as a foundation for using the twelve keys to expand your consciousness in order to prepare the way for an experience of your soul.

One way to encourage yourself to appreciate and love yourself more is to go beyond a feeling of being ordinary and unimportant, which is a feeling that we can all create at times. You will be able to love yourself more fully if you learn to view yourself as *a fascinating, multifaceted being with many admirable qualities and talents that you are in the process of uncovering and*

expressing in your life. You can learn to appreciate the *mystery* of yourself as a remarkable being who has been sent into earth life by your soul for very important purposes.

I think that most people believe that they know who they are. After all, they have been living with their human *self* for many years. Their self is familiar to them, and usually it is taken for granted because it is so familiar. But, for most people, what they know about their human self is just knowledge about the surface of their being. It is only knowledge about their conscious life in the physical world that they are quite familiar with, knowledge that they have gained through their ordinary awareness.

Many people are not aware that within their human self there is an incredible, wonderful, and magnificent underlying reality. They never become aware of that deeper aspect of their human self because they are so busy being the insignificant and unimportant person that they mistakenly believe they are. That prevents them from discovering that they have a second channel of Extraordinary Awareness. Perceiving themselves through that expanded awareness would show them the true magnificence of themselves as human beings.

From my many years of spiritual and psychological research, I am convinced that within every person, within their personality self structure—and even within those individuals who might manifest negative behaviors that we do not like—there are permanent qualities that you can think of as "energies" of extraordinary goodness and magnificence. Those beautiful energies have been placed into the personality structure of every living person by their soul.

We are all free to ignore those energies of goodness. We can even choose to believe that there are no such energies within us. However, no matter what we believe, *we cannot diminish the magnificent energies that are there at the core of our human self.*

I believe that one of the most important purposes of human life on earth is to bring our magnificent inner qualities to the surface and live them out in the physical world day after day. Your soul intends for you live your positive inner qualities through the daily expression of idealism, generosity, honesty, kindness, compassion, and love. Those are the *outer* expressions of the inner qualities of goodness that your soul has placed into your human personality structure.

On your path of enlightenment, it will be important for you to see yourself in terms of those qualities of *goodness*. If you do not see yourself in such a positive light, you might create your image of who you are based upon negative thoughts and feelings that you create about your personality self. You can understand that when you have such a negative picture of yourself, it will very difficult to love yourself.

One of the factors that will strongly influence the image that you create of yourself will be your perception of how well you are doing in your activities in the physical world. For example, if you are highly successful in your work and you are making a great deal of money, you will tend to feel more confident and therefore be more likely to have a positive image of who you are. If you are struggling in your work and not succeeding in reaching your goals, then you will tend to feel less worthy as a person.

Thus, generally speaking, when you have satisfying and fulfilling accomplishments in your life in the outer world that bring you joy, it will be easy to feel good about yourself. On the other hand, when you have negative results, you will usually feel bad about yourself. When you think deeply about these natural tendencies that we all have, you can realize that *your vision of yourself as a person is manipulated by physical circumstances.*

If you allow yourself to be constantly manipulated by physical circumstances—meaning that your affairs in the world must go well for you to feel that you are a good person—then you can become a "victim" of the complexities of the outer world. You can create a distorted perspective that will cause you to overlook the profound goodness that lives within your human self—a goodness that is always there, even when you have disappointments and failures in your life in the outer world. With that distorted perspective you will find it difficult to be aware of the extraordinary energies, talents, and abilities that have been placed into your human self by your soul.

As you work with the twelve keys to higher consciousness, you will need to remind yourself that the beautiful inner qualities of your human self do not *vanish* when you are unhappy about your life in the outer world, and then *suddenly return* when you feel pleased about what you are doing in daily life. Those inner qualities are a permanent part of your human self.

When your activities and relationships in the physical world are difficult, disappointing, or painful, it will be very helpful to take the attitude that you are simply having some temporary challenges that you will eventually work through. You can remind yourself that you have not suddenly become a bad person, or a failure in life. You can understand that challenges do not diminish the inherent goodness within you. You are still a worthy, wonderful human being, even when you are struggling in your life.

Everyone can have thoughts, feelings, or actions that they are not proud of, that they believe are wrong or bad. If you only focus on those negative aspects of your experience, you might come to believe that there is something wrong with you. Seeing yourself in that way can lead you to the attitude that when you *fix* all of the things that you believe are wrong with you, *then* you will be a good person. *Then*, you will be willing to feel love for your human self. Until then, you believe that you are not worthy of admiration and love, and you withhold it from yourself.

I see many people do this with their spouse, or their children, or their friends. If the people in their life continue to act in positive, pleasing ways, then they are willing to love those people. If those same people present difficult, negative behaviors, the love is withdrawn.

This tendency can be very obstructive as you try to

see your goodness and love yourself. That is because we all have become so proficient at finding flaws in ourselves. When we establish the habit of withholding love from ourselves because we see flaws that we have, then no matter how many positive changes we make, and no matter how much we grow, we seem to always find something else wrong with our human self that makes us feel that we are not yet worthy of our own love.

This seems to go on day after day, year after year. With this habit, we may never feel that we have fixed all of our flaws. As soon as we heal one thing, the harsh critic within us can find something else to criticize and condemn. I have worked with elderly people who have been doing this for 60, 70, even 80 years. They are good people, but they are still so busy finding something wrong with themselves that they continue to feel unworthy and unlovable.

There is something very important that you need to know. That is: *You can love your human self while you are working on the things that you do not like in your personality.* If you are willing to do that, then you will not need to wait until you think that you are perfect before you create love for yourself.

To help yourself here, you can say this to yourself as a reminder and as a positive affirmation:

> "I am a wonderful person, and, I am working to change some personality patterns that I do not like. While I am doing that, I affirm that I am going to love myself during the entire process of change and healing."

Loving yourself in this way will accelerate the transformation of the patterns in you that you want to change. It will enable you to remember, and *feel*, that you are a good person while you are making the changes in any thoughts, feelings, and behaviors that you believe need to be changed.

As you use the twelve keys to higher conscious to open your Extraordinary Awareness to gain an awareness of your soul, it will be important to create a vision of yourself as a wonderful person who is filled with goodness. You will need to consistently remind yourself that no matter what negative personality patterns you might manifest at times, they cannot diminish the inner goodness that has been placed into your human self by your soul. Your negative patterns simply temporarily obscure that true goodness, making it difficult at times for you to feel it, or believe in it.

As you move along on your path of enlightenment, even as you begin to pay more attention to loving yourself, you will notice that your vision of who you are can fluctuate from day to day. Some days you will feel very loving toward yourself and it will be easy for you to believe in your innate goodness—to believe that you are truly a good person. Then, at other times, the same old feelings of unworthiness can come back and you will feel bad about yourself. As long as you know that such fluctuations in your vision of yourself are *normal*, then you will not be too troubled by them.

You can keep reminding yourself that even though your thoughts and feelings about yourself can fluctuate from day to day, the *inner goodness* that pours into you from your soul is steady and permanent. As you remember that, it will enable you to focus more fully on the goodness within you when you are grappling with challenges in your day to day life.

If you have extended periods of emotional pain, or if you are struggling with disappointment in your activities or relationships in the physical world, you can learn to take some quiet time each day to let go of your difficulties and get back in touch with the permanent goodness inside yourself. You can use the daily attunement process that you will learn in this book to accomplish that. Using that process will help you stimulate a renewed love for yourself. It will also help you feel inspired and rejuvenated, and that will give you the confidence to deal more effectively with your challenges.

As you work with your thoughts and feelings each day to create a vision of yourself that is aligned with your true goodness, you will need to remember that no matter how bad you might be feeling about yourself at certain times, and no matter how frustrated you might be because you cannot *feel* your goodness at those times, you can always *say* or *think* the truth about that goodness by using a strong affirmative statement. Even if you cannot feel the truth of the statement in that moment, you can still say it to yourself, or you can think it. The power of the words can help lift you out of your distorted vision of yourself that you are creating during a challenging moment.

Here is a powerful statement that I have used

when I have forgotten the truth because I am caught up in my own negative thoughts and feelings:

> "My feelings are *temporary*. No matter what negative thoughts and feelings I am having about myself right now, the *truth* is that I am a magnificent human being. The truth is that there is a permanent, ongoing energy of *goodness* within me, placed there by my soul. My negative thoughts and feelings of this moment cannot diminish that goodness."

When you say the truth to yourself in this way, you will trigger deep unconscious patterns within you that are aligned with the energies of goodness that are streaming into your personality self from your soul. The more that you stir up those patterns, the sooner you will release the temporary negative illusion that you have created about yourself. As you release your self-created negativity, and as you create new loving thoughts and feelings about yourself, you will open the way for the powerful energies of goodness from your soul to come into your conscious awareness.

The more that you say this affirmative statement of truth to yourself, the more you can respond to the words with feelings of love for yourself. In time, as you train yourself, you will only need to begin to think this statement and the feelings of love will come bubbling up inside you.

You do not need to be continually manipulated by your negative thoughts and feelings about yourself. Those thoughts and feelings are flexible, and you can learn to change them. If you have a habit of creating self-diminishing thoughts and feelings, you can change that habit. Whenever you want, you can choose to practice releasing those negative thoughts and feelings, and then, using this affirmation, or other inspirational words, you can *create* loving thoughts and feelings about yourself that reflect the truth of your goodness, that match the true magnificence of your being.

At times, you can feel unworthy and bad about yourself as a result of outer events in your life. If someone treats you badly, or condemns you for some reason, it is natural to feel unsure or diminished. In those kinds of experiences, it is usually just a matter of living through the negative feelings about yourself until they go away. As you are caught up in the process of working through such feelings, you will not expect to feel a great deal of love for yourself.

After you get through the pain and suffering associated with negative experiences in the world, then you are free to take your thoughts and feelings in hand and lovingly remind yourself of the true goodness of your human self. You can say to yourself: "*My negative thoughts and feelings are temporary. They can never diminish the true goodness that lives within my human self.*" That can help you return to a vision of yourself as a worthy person, and that can lead you to a full healing of your painful thoughts and feelings that were caused by outer events in your life.

If you have a strong *habit* of being self-critical, you might find it difficult to create the feelings of love for yourself that are necessary to open to an awareness of your soul. To heal such a habit of self-criticism, it can be very effective to use the power of your *imagination*. You can use your imagination in the follow manner.

Every time that you notice that you are being harsh, critical, and unkind toward yourself, take a minute to sit in silence and begin to imagine yourself as a small, innocent, lovable child. Imagine that you are your own child. Create a deep feeling of love for the child. Know that this wonderful child will feel deeply hurt from your harsh treatment.

Since you do not want to hurt your child, in that moment, you let go of your criticism of the child—your criticism of yourself. You focus on your innocent child, and you imagine embracing the child with all the love that you can summon up from within you.

This simple technique can be extremely powerful in healing a habit of self-criticism and establishing a deeper sense of self love. Use it often and you will feel the beneficial changes that come in your attitude toward yourself.

Some people have trouble doing this technique because they focus so consistently on the negativity that they believe exists within their human self that they cannot feel like they are a good person. When they believe that they are filled with negativity, they cannot believe that there is any goodness within them. Naturally, they come to feel: "I am such a limited, unworthy person." They constantly go to the *negative* extreme in their attitude toward themselves.

If you are going to miscalculate in creating your picture of who you are as a human self, why not err on the *positive* side? You can say to yourself: "*I am an incredible person. I am a manifestation of the divine goodness of my soul expressing in human form.*" That would be much more beneficial than constantly telling yourself how limited and unworthy you are. And that would help you move forward on your path of enlightenment toward an awakening to the magnificence of your soul.

Chapter 5

The Second Key: Expanding Your Vision of Your Soul

---※---

As you work with the second key to higher consciousness, which is, *expanding your vision of your soul*, you can begin with the understanding that your beliefs that you hold about your soul—your concept of your soul—will be a major factor in determining whether or not you can consistently have a direct experience of your soul. A small, limited vision of your soul can block your inner opening, making it difficult for you to open your second channel of Extraordinary Awareness.

As I mentioned in Chapter Two, some people think of their soul as being limited like the human self.

They believe that the soul has to be nurtured, trained, or improved. I choose to take a different view. I believe that our souls are divine beings who are unlimited, perfect, and even *God*-like. This perspective has inspired me, and many of my students, to make a connection to our soul that has brought more of that perfection into our human experience.

If you have a vision of your soul as being human-like, then you must assume that your soul has the confusions and limitations of a human personality self. On the other hand, envisioning your soul as a perfect divine being who is not constrained by human limits will help you create a concept of your soul that will move you toward an experience of the true magnificence of your soul.

I suggest that you create a *large* vision of your soul that truly inspires you. If you are a Christian, you might say: "My soul is extraordinarily perfect. My soul exists beside the perfect soul of Jesus." If you are a Buddhist, you could say: "My soul is filled with the same radiant, divine perfection that shines forth from the Buddha." Whatever your orientation toward the spiritual realm might be, create the most *perfect* image of your soul that you can imagine. Whatever your highest spiritual ideals are, attribute them to your soul. In time, as you move along your path of enlightenment, you will discover that your soul truly has those vast, unlimited, and perfect qualities.

As a starting point for expanding your vision of your soul, you can use the ideas that I presented in Chapter Two. They can give you a solid base for awakening to an ever-expanding understanding of the true magnificence of your soul. They can also stimulate you to move from seeing your soul through your ordinary awareness, to perceiving it with your Extraordinary Awareness.

To help you build that base I will summarize for you eight important aspects of your soul, and its relationship to you as a human personality self, that were given in Chapter Two. Think of these often, and carry them with you in your heart. Try to feel the truth of them. You can build your expanded vision of your soul on these statements:

> 1. Your soul exists *beyond* the physical world, *beyond time and space*. Your soul is your wonderful, perfect, *true* being that penetrates *all* dimensions of reality.
>
> 2. Your soul is the incredible non-physical aspect of you that is *eternal*. Your soul existed *before your human birth* into this lifetime, and will continue to exist *after your physical death*.
>
> 3. You *are* your soul right now. While you are temporarily experiencing yourself as a human being in a physical body, you are also *simultaneously* existing as your soul in a non-physical, spiritual realm.
>
> 4. Your soul and your human personality self are not separate entities. There is no distance between yourself and your soul. Your soul is inside you. It is a part of your being.

5. Your soul is constantly loving you and encouraging you, never criticizing you or condemning you. Your soul walks every step of your human pathway with you. You are never alone on your journey.

6. Your soul is a vast inner reservoir of wisdom, courage, strength, creativity, talents, abilities, and answers to your questions about your life. You can learn to tap in to that reservoir to draw out what you need to fulfill yourself in your human life.

7. Your soul is your personal connection to the larger spiritual realities of life. It is your personal doorway to the eternal realm.

8. Your soul is continually involved in an ongoing cosmic creativity with all other souls, and with the all-encompassing, all-loving creative forces of life that manifest as God.

When you build your vision of your soul on these focal points, in time, as you carry out the process of personal enlightenment and you learn to perceive through your Extraordinary Awareness, you will be able to directly experience your soul as your wonderful, perfect, totally loving, true being that resides in the spiritual realm, but that also shares your human life with you.

It is important to realize that your human personality self is a temporary vehicle that you use to live your life inside your physical body. When your physical body dies, that personality self will be released from your body and it will be taken up into your soul.

Understanding this, you can now begin to create an expanded vision of your soul by entering into one of the greatest mysteries of existence. That mystery involves *the extraordinary journey of your soul, existing beyond time and space, but expressing in the human world from the beginning of time, until this present moment.*

As I pointed out earlier, your soul has drawn upon and manipulated the perfect, eternal creative forces of life in order to manifest your present unique human personality self structure of energies. Those energies have been placed into your physical body and they have become what you now experience as your human self. To begin the expansion of your vision of your soul, you will now need to understand that *since the beginning of human life on earth, you-as-a-soul have been creating such personality energy structures and placing them into human bodies.*

From my years of personal experience of the spiritual realm, and from thousands of spiritual readings that I have done as research to acquire information about the nature of the soul, I have come to understand that the soul of each of us is involved in a great cosmic journey through time and space. From their existence in the non-physical spiritual realm, the souls are projecting a portion of their soul-awareness as human self energy structures lifetime after lifetime on earth. This ongoing manifestation of our soul creates a remarkable sequence of human lives that each of us has lived on earth through the ages.

❖

Our popular literature is filled with accounts of people who remember past lifetimes. Of the tens of thousands of people that I have personally worked with through the years, I would estimate that at least twenty-percent of them are convinced that they have had a real experience of a past lifetime.

In my own life, when I was in my twenties, the concept of past lifetimes was just an interesting idea to me. Then, after having several powerful and dramatic waking experiences of my own past lifetimes that were just as real as my normal experiences in daily life, the concept of past lifetimes became a living reality for me.

To expand your vision of your soul, it can be very helpful to begin to think of *yourself* as your soul, expressing through many different human beings that you have been in many lifetimes in the past. Imagining the vast scope and richness of such experiences through the ages will help you to feel that you are truly an important spiritual being who is pursuing many important purposes on earth. Even if you cannot yet become *consciously* aware of your past lifetimes to remember what those purposes were, by imagining that you have been pursuing great purposes through many lifetimes, you will be able to trust that your present life is an extension of those important purposes. You will be able to feel that there are important purposes in your present life, even if you cannot yet say exactly what they are.

We are all living our present lifetime in a way that has to do with personal accomplishments that we achieved in past lifetimes. Those accomplishments are now being brought into our present lifetime to be built upon and extended. When you understand this you will be able to feel that your *true* existence through time is much more than what you are aware of as a single individual in your present life. You will eventually realize that your present life is adding greatly to your human achievements through many lifetimes, and those achievements will eventually accumulate in a way that will lead you to the *mastery* of the human world.

As you move along on your path of enlightenment, in time, you will come to know that human life and death are temporary cycles of existence that *you-as-a-soul* pass through on your way to mastery of the physical world. When you learn to perceive consistently through your Extraordinary Awareness, you will eventually come to know that your existence through many human lifetimes in time and space is an ongoing expression that is actually taking place within the perfect non-physical reality of the cosmic eternal love energy that exists beyond time and space.

Using the twelve keys to expand your awareness can eventually lead you to an experience of the ultimate truth of life, which is: *Life is eternal.* At the death of your present physical body, the inner life that your present human self is now living will go forward to express in ways that are intimately woven with divine souls who are manifestations of the eternal creative forces of life.

You can understand the manifestation of *you-as-a-soul* through many human lifetimes as a *progression* through the physical world of time and space that has the purpose of mastering the human world *from within*. For greater inspiration, and for an even more expanded vision of your soul, you can see the progression of your own personal sequence of human lives on earth in the context of *the evolution of humanity through time*. To help you see that, I will briefly summarize a vast amount of metaphysical knowledge that I have gained through the years that you can use to stimulate your thinking and feeling about the extraordinary human drama that you, and all of us, are participating in as emissaries sent into earth life by our souls who stand in the eternal realm sharing the journey with us.

I believe that at the beginning of the human journey on earth, in the initial stages of human life, the souls projected the human selves into physical bodies in such a perfect way that all people experienced a pure love for one another. They clearly perceived that they were joined to one another by that universal love. The clear and predominant experience of all people was that they belonged with everyone else. There was not the sense of a separate individuality, but the sense of being a part of the entire human group, the entire human race.

Gradually, as humans evolved, there came to be a strong focus upon the feeling of being a single individual. People began to experience a unique *individuality*. Rather than feeling dominated by the experience of feeling that they were part of the human group, people began to experience themselves predominantly as an individual *self*.

For ages, humans built creatively upon the new

experience of the self and its individuality. Eventually, that brought about the manifestation of the strong human "ego." I am using the word *ego* in the *positive* sense to indicate the joy that we can have when we fully value and love our individual self.

However, over a long period of time, too much focus on the individual self created a strong selfishness in many people that began to dominate their human experience. This led to challenges between individuals and groups that eventually created a general experience of separation from others.

Because of the separation that arose in humanity through time, there came to be a need for individuals to re-learn the sensitivity to other people that humans had in the beginning stages of life on earth, but that was generally lost in the development of the individual ego. There needed to be the regaining of the love for others, as well as a reawakening of the experience of belonging to the human group. If the experience of *belonging to all of humanity* could then be integrated with the strong sense of *the individual self*, then there could be the full and complete expression of human life on earth.

It seems to me that at the present time, most people are strongly focused on their *self*—their strong personal experiences, as well as the personal desires that they are trying to fulfill in the physical world. Yet, many people are clearly attempting to integrate into their own personal quest for fulfillment, a love for other people. This appears to be the period in which many people are instinctively involved in the present evolutionary step that humanity is now passing through—a step that involves bringing together a love of self with a love of other people.

The steps in the human evolutionary process are being taken by all people through many lifetimes. We are all progressing through the human cycles of life on earth at our own pace. I believe that for those who are eager to more forward more rapidly, the key is to continue the expression of our individual self in a strong manner, while integrating that with a love for others and the re-creation of the experience of belonging to the entire human group. Then, for the greatest completion of the purposes that our soul is pursuing through time, what we can add to that is an awakening of a conscious experience of our soul and the spiritual realm. That would truly be a merging of the *human* and the *divine* within our experience on earth.

Whenever you have a private moment during the day, sit in a quiet relaxation and try to imagine the vast journey of your soul as I have described it for you. Such periods of silent attunement will continue the expansion of your vision of your soul, will help you open your second channel of Extraordinary Awareness, and will stimulate your process of awakening to the true reality of your soul. You will move toward an experience of sharing the profound joy and love of the spiritual realm with your soul, and with the extraordinary creative forces of life. During those silent periods, let yourself soar into a world without limit. A world so filled with love that you feel inspired and uplifted from simply imagining it.

As you carry out this inner attunement, imagine the incredible love energies of the spiritual realm pouring into your human self. Create a feeling of deep connection with that beautiful divine reality. Then, as you move on with your process of enlightenment day after day, you will eventually come to *know*, through your own experience, that you are *never* apart from the magnificent spiritual reality of your soul. And that knowing will bring you great joy in your daily life.

Chapter 6

The Third Key: Changing Limited Thought Patterns

---- ✵ ----

The third key to higher consciousness is: *Changing your limited thought patterns.* This involves working with the tremendous power of your mind to recognize how you have limited your spiritual awakening by creating thoughts about yourself and about life that diminish your experience of yourself as a person. You will learn to use the power of your mind in creative new ways that will help you to change those limited patterns so that they do not stand in the way of opening your second channel of Extraordinary Awareness. This will be an important step forward on your path of enlightenment.

Each thought that you create exercises the power of your mind in one way or another. You can use that power to create limited, distorted thoughts that can bring pain and suffering into your life. Or, you can create thoughts that reflect the true goodness of you as a human self, and as an eternal soul. Those inspiring thoughts can bring joy and love into your day to day experience.

The thoughts that you *consistently* create about life will determine the *quality* of your human experience. If your thoughts are small and narrow, your experience will be unsatisfying. If you expand your thoughts, your human experience can begin to reflect the true vastness and beauty of life.

Everyone creates a certain *foundation of beliefs* about life, based on their persistent thoughts. Some people focus a great deal on negative thoughts about life. So, their basic belief is that life is essentially bad. Others who are able to create consistent positive thoughts about life create a basic belief in the goodness of life.

Of course, we all continually fluctuate back and forth between positive and negative thoughts, just as we can fluctuate between our first and second channel of awareness. But, in our thoughts, we have some fairly consistent mental patterns that we build as habits through the years. If those habitual thought patterns are essentially negative, then we will limit ourselves and our awareness. If we can create positive thoughts on a consistent basis, then we will open the door to a beautiful and satisfying experience of life.

When you experience your basic beliefs about life, it is important to understand that your thoughts are not truths about life. They are only temporary human creations. Some thoughts can *reflect* the truth, while others can be very distorted and far from the truth.

If you constantly think that human life is meaningless and without purpose, you can continue to believe that to be true throughout your life. Such thoughts will probably bring you a lot of sadness, yet they will not change the underlying goodness of all of life.

When you die, you will gradually peel away the illusion created by such distorted thoughts. You will see that during your human life, all the while that you were creating thoughts that life was meaningless, and accepting those thoughts as the truth, life itself was quite magnificent and filled with important purposes and meanings. You simply missed that magnificence because you were focused on your confused thoughts about meaninglessness. Because of your distorted thoughts, you missed the opportunity to have the true, fulfilling experience of life.

The way in which you use your thoughts will determine the vision of reality that you create. In a simple way of looking at this, you can imagine your mind as a camera that you can focus on anything. What you focus on is imprinted on the film, which develops into your picture of the world.

On your path of enlightenment, it will be important to take an honest, objective look at your basic, *consistent* thoughts about life. If you assess those thought patterns and discover that, in general, even though you might have some occasional negative thoughts, your thoughts about life are essentially positive, then you can assume that your beliefs about life are a relatively clear reflection of truth, for the *real* nature of all life is harmony and goodness, no matter what negativity might temporarily appear from the human point of view. On the other hand, if your thoughts are essentially negative, you are misperceiving the harmonious and loving nature of the underlying spiritual energies of life.

What is so vital for you to understand is that you can willfully choose the thoughts that you consistently focus upon. You can choose to focus on positive thoughts that reflect the true nature of yourself and life, and that will help you move toward the awakening of your Extraordinary Awareness.

If you do not choose to direct your thoughts toward the truth—toward harmony, honesty, idealism, and love—then such thoughts may not arise by themselves. That is because we all have a strong "animal" tendency that is inherent in the structure of the physical body that influences us to rush toward pleasure and flee from pain. This is a basic instinct shared by all animals and by all humans. It is intended to lead you to care for your body and protect it from physical harm. And, it is usually a beneficial influence to follow in relation to your physical body. However, when this animal tendency is carried over into your thoughts, it can be quite confusing.

Under the strong influence of this instinctive tendency to embrace pleasure and avoid pain, you can become preoccupied with your thoughts about personal gratification. That will begin to exaggerate a tendency toward selfishness that is inherent in our animal nature. If that occurs, most of your thoughts will be focused on yourself. You will not naturally think about other people, about being kind to them. You will not create thoughts of idealism and goodness. You will just pay attention to what pleases you and what leads to your own gratification. Thus, if you do not *choose* thoughts about goodness and idealism, your thoughts can often drift into selfishness and negativity.

If you consistently choose creative, positive, and inspiring thoughts about life, then your experiences will begin to blossom in more joyful, more beautiful, more creative, and more satisfying ways. That will lead to experiences that are a clearer reflection of the underlying truth of life.

I once worked with a woman, Kathy, who constantly criticized her husband. She kept creating more and more negative thoughts about him. Even though he was a kind, sensitive man, she focused so much on her negative thoughts about him that she began to withdraw from him emotionally. Finally, she felt that she could not tolerate being with him and she decided that she would need to get a divorce.

I gave Kathy a plan for helping her *choose* different thoughts about her husband. As part of that plan, each morning, as soon as she woke up, she said to herself: "My thoughts are not truths. They are temporary. I can change them. I now affirm that throughout this day, I will create positive thoughts about my husband."

And she did. Any time that she noticed the old negative thoughts, she let them go. Then, she created positive thoughts to replace them. In a matter of weeks, she felt a change come over her. She began to open emotionally to her husband, and she started to feel closer to him. He even started to seem more attractive and desirable to her. In time, she brought the love alive again. She accomplished all of that through the creative work that she did with the power of her thoughts.

You can learn to change your narrow, limited thought patterns. That will free you to open your Extraordinary Awareness to move forward in your work with the twelve keys to awaken to an experience of your soul.

There is a simple process that you can use to change your limited thoughts. First, you will need to honestly, but lovingly, identify the limited thoughts that you consistently create. Observe yourself for a while in a kind, objective way. When you notice any consistent limited thought patterns, bring them to your attention and examine them to see them more clearly.

For example, imagine that in observing the thoughts that you have about expanding your consciousness to experience your soul, you notice that you consistently create the thought: "It is too difficult to expand my consciousness, I cannot do it." Obviously, such a thought will block your progress.

To work with such a limited thought pattern, you could spend some time each day sitting in silence to bring that thought into your mind. For a few minutes, simply have the thought: "It is too difficult to expand my consciousness, I cannot do it." *Accept* that thought. Experience it fully for a few minutes.

Then, take a few deep breaths, relax your body,

and say to yourself: "This thought about being limited in my ability to expand my consciousness is *only* a thought. *It is not a truth.*"

Then, say the truth to yourself. In this example, you could say this to yourself:

> "The *truth* is that I have a great inner power given to me by my soul with which I can expand my human awareness. I *do* have the ability within me to go beyond my present limited human awareness to experience my soul. These are the thoughts that I now *choose* to create for myself."

This kind of statement is an affirmation—a formal statement of positive thoughts that you can use to focus on what you wish to accomplish. You can create such affirmations to focus the power of your mind in any area of your life that is important to you. For example, if you are trying to be more patient in your daily life, you might say this kind of statement to yourself as an affirmation: "I have a deep ability to manifest patience. I choose to use that ability now to create a feeling of being patient."

When you create your affirmations to focus the power of your mind where you wish that power to be directed, what is important is to choose words and ideas for your affirmative statements that free you from limits and move you toward a larger experience of reality. If you notice that you tend to feel that you must frame your affirmative statements in the context of present limits that you believe that you have in your life—limits that have come about as you have used only your first channel of ordinary awareness throughout your life—then boldly go against that and create your affirmations with the feeling that you are free to say *anything* to your mind that will help you feel the vast reservoir of talents and abilities that you have within your human self—treasures that have been placed there by your soul.

When you are working to create such positive, inspiring thoughts, it is very important not to slip into a feeling that your negative, limiting thoughts are *bad*. If you have some negative thoughts, accept them, experience them, and then *release* them. Know that such negative thoughts are temporary, and they cannot damage your being. Then go ahead and create the strong positive thoughts that you wish to use as affirmations to focus the power of your mind.

As you use positive affirmations to progress in your spiritual awakening, you may occasionally create strong doubts about some of your spiritual beliefs. If you immediately assume that those doubts mean that your beliefs are untrue, you will do yourself a great disservice. At that point, it will be important to remind yourself that doubts are only thoughts, and all thoughts are temporary. You can simply experience your doubting thoughts, think them through, asses them for what they can tell you, then release them—"vent" them.

Then, after you vent your doubts, calmly turn your intelligence toward the spiritual beliefs that you were doubting and examine them objectively to see if you now believe that they are still meaningful and beneficial for you. That kind of calm assessment will help you decide if you wish to keep your present spiritual beliefs that you were doubting, or if you need to change them.

For example, imagine that as a child you believed in "elves." You instinctively shifted to your Extraordinary Awareness without knowing it and you actually saw elves cavorting about in the forest. Then, as an adult trained in the present scientific view of life that is restricted to the first channel of ordinary awareness, you doubt your belief in elves. Before you decide the truth about your childhood experience of elves, you can enter your doubts, examine them, and look to find any underlying *fears* that might be causing you to create doubting thoughts.

When you do that, you might find that you are afraid that if you believe in elves, you will be seen as an unintelligent person. In that case, you would simply work with your fear of being seen as unintelligent and heal it.

After that, you could say: "It is now time to objectively decide the issue of elves for myself." Without the fear of being seen as an unintelligent person, you thoroughly study the issue of elves. In that study you discover that throughout the ages human beings have believed in many non-physical beings, such as elves, fairies, gnomes, angelic beings, and gods. As you view that objectively, you might come to this conclusion: "I choose to believe in certain divine forces that as a child I perceived as elves. Now that I have gained more experience in life, I now choose to believe that those divine forces that I perceived are actually energies from my soul that my child self unknowingly translated into visions of elves."

In this example, there are many different conclusions that you could come to about your beliefs. The important point here is that you are *choosing* what to believe according to an intelligent use of the power of your mind. You are not being coerced into giving up important spiritual beliefs simply because your mind created some temporary doubts about those important beliefs.

For various reasons that have to do with our own unique experience of life, we have all learned to create thoughts that limit our full potential to love our human self, and to awaken to the majesty of our existence as a soul. As you learn to manage and direct the power of your mind with intelligence and sensitivity, you will be able to recognize habits of limited thinking that you have created through the years, and you will find ways to change your limited thoughts so that you can direct the power of your mind toward new thoughts about yourself that will inspire you and help you feel the true goodness of your human self and your soul. That wise use of the power of your mind will be one of the most important aspects of awakening to a conscious awareness of your soul, and it will help you move toward the personal enlightenment that you will achieve by using the twelve keys to higher consciousness.

Chapter 7

The Fourth Key: Mastering Your Expectations

---- ✻ ----

You have now come to the fourth key to higher consciousness, which is: *Mastering your expectations*. In this inner work you will learn to notice what you *expect* to happen when you enter a silent period of attunement to practice awakening to your soul. Then, you will learn how to make some inner adjustments that will enable you to release any unrealistic and limiting expectations about what you believe you *should* experience as you begin to expand your awareness. This will be very important in freeing yourself from those expectations so that they do not become an obstacle on your path of enlightenment.

For example, as you begin to open your second channel of Extraordinary Awareness, if you expect to experience your soul as a solid, three-dimensional angelic being standing in your room with you, and that does not happen, then you will feel that you are failing in your attempt to expand your consciousness. However, you could actually be expanding your consciousness quite successfully in a more subtle way, but you would not notice that because you were looking for an angelic being to appear in front of you as you expected you should.

Since your soul is not a physical being, your perception of your soul may not be a perception that you become aware of through your physical senses of sight, sound, touch, taste, or smell. Some people who learn to experience their soul do occasionally have a fairly tangible sensory experience of the soul, such as a vision, but for most people, the experience is usually much more intangible than a vision of an angelic being. Therefore, if you were expecting to see such a being with your physical eyes, you would be so strongly focused on that expectation that you would not notice the subtle, non-physical manifestation of your soul that was occurring in that moment. Your expectation would be standing in the way of your spiritual unfoldment.

Even after you do begin to have an occasional inner sensing of your soul, your expectations about how that experience should be conceptualized can cause you some confusion. For example, in the early years of my own spiritual search, as I did a simple meditation practice each day, when I would have a vague sense of the presence of "something spiritual," I would later think about that in terms of some rather naive beliefs about the spiritual realm that I had at that time. Those beliefs came from a *scientific* attitude that I had about the nature of reality.

At that time in my life, I was used to thinking about the spiritual realm as being located beyond earth in outer space. And, because my ideas about outer space were based on abstract scientific theories about the cosmos, and particularly influenced by images that we have all absorbed from telescopic photos of outer space, I would think of the spiritual realm as some kind of "energy" reality existing among the lifeless planets and stars that to me were lost in the blackness, coldness, and emptiness of the physical universe.

With that kind of expectation about what I would experience, as I began to shift to my second channel of Extraordinary Awareness, even as I managed to have an occasional inner sensing of the presence of my soul, instead of experiencing my soul as the warm, loving, nurturing force that I later discovered it to be, I felt that somehow my soul was part of that cold cosmic void that I thought of as the spiritual realm. As a result, I felt a sense of uneasiness when I had my initial consciousness expanding experiences. I was hesitant to open myself to a spiritual presence that seemed to be cold and foreign.

Of course, that was just my distorted imagination based on my confused expectations. As I worked through that confusion and was able to release those distortions, I gradually came to experience the presence of my soul as the wonderful force of warmth and love that it truly is.

We all tend to have expectations about what we will experience as we open to the spiritual realm. In your work with the twelve keys, you will need to be alert to unrealistic or obstructive expectations, like the ones that I had during my "scientific" period. You will need to establish a habit of monitoring your expectations.

For me, it took a while to work through several "cycles" of unrealistic expectations. When I realized that my vision of the spiritual realm existing in the cold cosmic void of outer space was limiting me, I began to free myself from that vision by reading books about the spiritual experiences of other people. I especially enjoyed reading about spiritual masters and gurus who reported having amazing experiences of clairvoyance, knowledge of the future, clear visions of the spiritual realm, and other astounding mystical experiences.

After reading so many of those stories, I began to expect that when I did my meditation each day I should have similar experiences. For months, when I meditated, I expected to have the kind of dramatic mystical experiences that I had read about. However, each day as I meditated, to my disappointment, I only had simple feelings of relaxation and peace. There were no mystical experiences.

As that continued on day after day, I naturally believed that I was *failing* in my meditation practice. Since I was expecting dramatic experiences, when they did not happen, then I assumed that I was not having a spiritual experience As a result, I began to "try" to meditate. I would try to push my inner experience toward the mystical experiences that I expected I should have when I meditated. That created an inner tension that actually prevented me from releasing myself into the spiritual experience that I was trying so hard to have.

After months of struggling with myself, I got very frustrated and discouraged about my meditation practice. I was so unhappy about not achieving the mystical experiences that I expected to have that I began to feel that meditating was a waste of time. I almost gave up and quit meditating.

Eventually, I came to realize that my problem was my unrealistic expectations about what I should experience in meditation. It became clear to me that if I did not *expect* to have dramatic mystical experiences when I meditated, then I would not feel disappointed when they did not occur. If I could let go of that expectation, then I could enjoy whatever happened when I meditated. So, all that I needed to do in order to go on with my meditation practice was to release my expectations about what a meditation experience should be.

In my work to release my expectations I created a simple affirmation. I said this affirmation at the beginning of each meditation:

> "In this moment, I let go of *all* expectations about what is supposed to happen as I release myself into a feeling of peace and calm. As I enter into this meditation, I open my heart, and I invite my soul to bring to me whatever experience I need."

❖

As I practiced in this way day after day, I was eventually able to release all expectations about what I should experience during meditation. I simply enjoyed the peaceful feelings that I had, and the pleasant, but rather "empty" experience of not being aware of anything tangible as I meditated.

After I had used that approach for a while, to my surprise, my simple "empty" experience began to take on a new quality. Since I was not busy looking for a dramatic mystical experience and feeling disappointed when I did not have one, I began to notice that I was having some vague, almost imperceptible experiences of warmth and pleasantness each time that I did my meditation. At times I would even sense that there was something wonderful, but "invisible," there with me in the "emptiness" of my meditation experience. It seemed to appear at the edges of my awareness, not directly in front of my inner vision.

In time, after I became more practiced at releasing my expectations during meditation, I began to experience a vague feeling of love that seemed to be coming from something beyond myself. However, that experience was very subtle, hardly noticeable. Had I been busy looking for a dramatic mystical experience, I never would have noticed that almost "unnoticeable" feeling of love. That experience would have been invisible to me when I was caught up in my dramatic expectations.

As I practiced becoming aware of that vague new experience of love in my daily meditations, I began to have a sense that in my experience there was something that was almost like an inner "opening." That opening was more of a feeling, rather than an actual visual image. Yet, it was a real opening that seemed like a passageway made of something like light. It was so subtle that had I been focused on my earlier dramatic expectations, I would have missed it.

I did not try to hold on to the new experience, or try to make it stronger. I just allowed myself to gently float toward that almost invisible opening of subtle light. I never seemed to pass through the opening, but I experienced a gentle feeling of love each time that I became aware of the opening.

Every day as I meditated, I had the subtle experience of the opening of light and the love. Then, eventually, I felt myself pass through that spiritual opening. On the other side, even though I had no visual image of what was there, the feeling of love was deeper. And, as I went through that inner passageway day after day in my meditations, my experience of love gradually grew stronger. After a while, those meditation experiences brought me powerful impressions of my soul loving me and guiding me.

Through the years, as I have learned to open my second channel of Extraordinary Awareness more and more, what began as a very subtle, almost imperceptible experience, has become an incredible experience of love and spiritual enlivenment. However, it took quite a bit of practice in releasing my expectations to open to such a deep experience.

As you use the twelve keys to create a daily attunement practice, the spiritual experiences that you have will be uniquely yours. You will not need to try to decide ahead of time what kind of experiences you will have. By releasing your expectations about what those unique experiences *should be*, you will prepare the way for allowing the experiences to be what they *need to be* for you. You will open the door to eventually experiencing your soul and the spiritual realm in a way that is best for your particular personality self.

I have worked with many people to help them open their second channel of Extraordinary Awareness, and the majority of them have had subtle experiences. Very few of them have encountered full-color, three-dimensional visions of their soul and the spiritual realm. Most experienced their soul in vague impressions and feelings that at first were almost imperceptible. Then, as they expanded their awareness, those feeling experiences deepened and became more impactful and inspiring.

It is rare for someone to have dramatic and vivid perceptions of the spiritual realities early in their attunement practice. So, if you expect that, you may miss the more subtle way in which your soul is communicating with you. That is why it is so important to release your expectations about what your spiritual experience should be so that you can allow that experience to be what it needs to be for you personally.

Also, if you become involved in a search for dramatic experiences in your inner work, even if you do create some visions and strong tangible perceptions of inner phenomena, you can become caught up in those experiences. You can become so attached to such experiences that you will not be able to see whether or not they are being created by your fantasy and wishful thinking. If they are, they could mislead you in your inner work. They could cause you to believe that you are perceiving truths about your soul and the spiritual realm, when you are actually caught up in your self-created fantasies.

Even after you begin to have deep, genuine spiritual experiences during your attunement periods, you will still need to work with your expectations because you will begin to expect to achieve that depth every day. It is important to recognize that the depth of your attunement experience can vary from day to day. One day you may have a very profound experience, and the next day you might feel like nothing meaningful is happening.

What is so important to know is that when you feel like you are not experiencing your soul, you are actually getting ready to break through to an even more subtle level of experience than you have known before. By allowing yourself to continue to release your expectations of what your attunement experience should be, you will be able to attune to even more subtle ways that your soul is loving you and guiding you.

So, do not underestimate the subtle signals. You may be heading toward experiences beyond anything that you might have expected or considered possible.

Remind yourself that expectations are *human*. Your soul is *divine*, and it can guide you in divine ways that your human personality self cannot anticipate.

I advise you to release your expectations and do your inner work with an innocent heart so that your soul can present itself to your awareness in its own way that is best for your human self. That approach will be the perfect complement to the other openings and adjustments that you will make on your path of personal enlightenment.

Chapter 8

The Fifth Key: Engaging Your Life In the Present Moment

---- ❈ ----

From the previous chapters, you have gained some knowledge about using your mind in a more enlightened way. Now, you are ready for the fifth key to higher consciousness, which is: *Engaging your life in the present moment.* This involves a patient, steady process of becoming aware of where you put your *attention* in your day to day life, and learning to make more beneficial choices about what you choose to focus upon.

Many people spend so much time focusing on the past, and planning for the future, that even when they are doing something important in the present moment, they do not put their full attention upon that. Thus, they often allow the present moment to slip away without deeply appreciating it and fully living it. They do not engage the *now* with enough intensity.

If they continue such a pattern through the years, the result can be a gradual numbing of their sensitivity to life. When that becomes a habit, even if they want to fully engage the present moment, they find it difficult to do.

As I have previously discussed, when you begin to attune to your soul, it will be necessary to learn to shift your attention from your first channel of ordinary awareness, to your second channel of Extraordinary Awareness. When you sit in the silence of your attunement period, if you are thinking about the past or the future, your attention will be locked into ordinary awareness. To shift to your Extraordinary Awareness, you will need to bring your attention to *the present moment*.

To be completely successful in awakening to your soul and the spiritual realm, you will need to learn to focus squarely on your experience in the present moment, without your attention wandering to the past or the future. For, *it is in the present moment that your awareness will expand. Now* is where your power lies. So, by practicing paying attention to your experience of the now, present moment in daily life, you can become adept at remaining focused on the present, and that will enable you to bring that ability forward to eventually have a deep spiritual experience during your attunement period.

The present moment is the doorway to your soul. When you are making your attunement, you do it in the present moment. You can think about doing another attunement tomorrow, which is in the future, but in that moment you will only be thinking, not engaging your soul in that moment. It is in the present moment that you will experience your soul, not in the past or in the future.

Your soul exists in *the eternal now*, so *now* is what is important in your work to experience your soul. You cannot live in the past. You can only remember it. And the future is merely a *concept* that we humans create within the context of *time*. We carry that concept in our minds to think about and talk about the moments that we are going to be living later on, in time. However, when we eventually get through time to those "future" moments that we were thinking about, they will then be our *present* as we are living out those moments.

Once you understand this, you will realize that *everything that occurs in our inner experience actually occurs in the present moment*. And, *the present moment for us humans, living within the context of time, actually exists* **within the eternal now, beyond time***, and that is the realm of the souls that love us and guide us.*

Throughout each day, as you carry out your important activities and relationships in the outside world, you can practice focusing on your experience in the present moment. You can direct your attention fully to whatever you are doing in the physical world. You can pay close attention to every person that you interact with in each present moment.

Naturally, as you do all of that, you will think about the past or the future in order to have continuity in your affairs, and in order to make plans for what you desire to do in the "future." Yet, even as you integrate your various thoughts about the past or the future into your daily experience, you can still train yourself to pay attention to *now*, no matter what you are doing. By doing that you will be able to live all of those now moments with an intense, passionate engagement. And, if you practice paying full attention to the now moments of your daily life, then you will find that it will be easier to bring the now moment into focus during your attunement periods.

Years ago, when I first began practicing fully engaging the present moment, my greatest challenge was *remembering* to do it during the day. It is not so difficult to bring your attention fully to the present moment when you remember that that is what you desire to do. But, if your experience is like mine was, when you first start this practice, you will usually be so caught up in distracting thoughts—some about the past or future—that you will not pay full attention to what you are doing, or who you are with in the present moment.

Even after I found ways to remind myself each day that I wanted to focus on the present moment in my daily experiences, I still occasionally sabotaged the process. One of the more humorous experiences of sabotage occurred when I was a student in graduate school.

At that time I had very little money, so I was careful about not buying anything that I did not really need. The one indulgence that I allowed myself was some very expensive herbal tea that was imported from England by a local health food store. I saved that tea for special occasions, and I was particularly mindful of paying close attention to the present moment when I drank the tea. I always tried to fully savor it.

One Christmas break in the university classes, I made arrangements to go on a special meditation retreat at a nearby monastery. Not only was I looking forward to the opportunity to practice deepening my meditation experience in the peaceful, rural setting of the monastery, but I thought that I would get a lot of practice staying in the present moment because there would be none of the usual distractions there—no telephones, radios, or television sets. (This was before people had personal computers.)

So, on the morning of my departure for the monastery, I was so delighted with my plans for the week that I decided to toast myself with a cup of my expensive tea. Practicing staying in the present moment, I carefully prepared my precious tea in a slow, Zen-like manner. As I took the first sip, I made a promise to myself that all during the week at the monastery I would pay attention to the present moment, just as I had when I prepared my tea. I began to imagine how I would do that. I saw myself walking in nature and looking closely at the sky, every tree, everything else, fully engaging my experience of it without letting my attention wander away from the present moment.

After a while, I noticed that my cup that had been

filled with my precious tea was now empty. With a shock, I realized that all the while that I had been planning how I was going to stay in the present moment when I got to the monastery, I had been sipping my tea. Now it was gone, and my awareness had been so far from the present moment that I had not even tasted my tea.

Although this is a simple, humorous example of how I sabotaged myself in my process of learning to live in the now, perhaps it will show you how easy it can be to get distracted when you are trying to remember to pay attention to your present moments. You will need to be alert and create your own methods for training yourself to stay in the present moment.

As you go through your daily activities, you can use simple techniques to help you remember to engage the present moment. For example, you might write words such as these on a small card: "*Now* is where my power lies. In this moment I bring my full attention to what I am doing and experiencing. I fully engage my life in this moment." Carry that card with you, and take it out and read it several times a day. That will help you remember to use your ability to live fully and intensely in the present whenever you desire to do that.

Another simple way to bring your attention into the present moment is to focus on your body. Whenever you have the opportunity during the day, sit quietly, take a deep breath, relax, and begin to bring your full attention to your body. What are your hands doing? Does your body feel warm or cool? Notice your feet. How do they feel? Notice how good it feels to let go of all of the distractions of daily life and be fully present in the now, enjoying being a human with a body that enables you to live your life on earth.

You can also learn to use a certain *feeling* as a trigger to shift your attention from the past or future into the present moment. For example, imagine that you are sitting in a beautiful park, and instead of engaging the beauty of the park in that moment, you realize that you are thinking about what you are going to do when you go home—just as I was thinking about how I was going to stay in the present moment when I got to the monastery.

In that moment, as you become aware that your attention has strayed from the present, you can take a deep breath, relax your body, and focus your attention on a beautiful tree in the park. Then, with your eyes on that tree, you can begin to create a feeling of letting go and *releasing* everything that you have been thinking about—releasing all of the thoughts that have been occupying your attention and preventing you from experiencing the beauty of the tree in the present moment. You can imagine that you are letting those distracting thoughts drop away, as if you have been carrying something very heavy, and you just let it go and drop it. In the same way, you can create a strong feeling of letting go, of releasing everything in your mind as you look at the beautiful tree.

As you work with this kind of *feeling of release*, combined with a sense of relaxation, you will be able to turn your attention away from everything but the visual focal point of the tree. As you focus your full attention on the tree, and you inwardly create the feeling of release, of letting go of everything, you will be creating an intense experience of the present moment.

If you consistently practice such a feeling of release, combined with a visual focal point of your choosing, after a while, you will become adept at creating that powerful focus on the present moment at will. Then, whenever you want to bring your attention to the present moment, you can simply close your eyes, call up your visual image, and create the feeling of release.

Each day, try to remember that the *present* is where your power lies. The *now* moment is where your soul lives. It is in some present moment *within time* that you will have an experience of becoming one with your soul *beyond time*.

Practice engaging the present moment in your daily life so that you can have deeper, more meaningful, and more satisfying experiences in the outside world. Then, as you use the twelve keys to create a rich inner life through a daily attunement program, you will be adept at fully engaging your experience in the present moment, and therefore you can have a more intense and satisfying experience of your attunement moments. Those deepened experiences will be a solid foundation upon which you will build your experience of your soul.

Chapter 9

The Sixth Key: Practicing Expanding Your Awareness

———— ✣ ————

With the preparation that you have made up to this point by working with the previous keys, you are ready to go to the sixth key to higher consciousness, which is: *Practicing the expansion of your conscious awareness.* This is a process of learning to expand your awareness in order to go beyond the limits of your ordinary perceptions of the physical world.

Working with this key, and with an advanced attunement method that I will give you in a later chapter, you can become aware of more than what appears in your physical reality at any given moment. You will be able to sense deeper purposes and meanings than what you usually perceive in ordinary physical events. You will become aware that there are magnificent non-physical realities that underlie the manifestation of the physical world, and you will be able to experience how your soul participates in the events and circumstances of your life.

You will accomplish this by practicing shifting your attention from your first channel of ordinary awareness to your second channel of Extraordinary Awareness. By consistently practicing the attunement methods that I will give you in this chapter, you can begin the process of awakening your Extraordinary Awareness to perceive many hidden spiritual realities that are affecting you in the now moment. Then, the advanced attunement method presented later will launch you more fully into your Extraordinary Awareness in a way that will move you further along on your path of enlightenment.

Learning to shift from your ordinary awareness to your Extraordinary Awareness will enable you to enter new "places" inside you that are different from what you are used to in your daily life. This is as though you come into a museum every day and you only go to the sculpture exhibit. After a while, you forget that there is anything else in the museum. All that you are aware of is the sculpture room. If you want to see some paintings, first, you have to remember that the museum *has* a painting room. Then, you have to go to that room. You will not see any paintings if you stay in the sculpture room. You will need to *extend* your experience in order to go beyond your habitual patterns of awareness.

The sculpture room in the museum represents your ordinary perception of the physical reality of daily life. The painting room represents the perception of the non-physical reality of your soul. To see paintings, you need to leave the sculpture room and go to the painting room. To perceive your soul, you need to leave your ordinary awareness that is immersed in the ongoing experience of daily life in the physical world and shift to your Extraordinary Awareness that is aligned with the *non*-physical reality where your soul exists.

You can use a simple process of attunement as your beginning point for learning to shift from your ordinary awareness to your Extraordinary Awareness. By practicing this process each day, you will eventually be able to use it as a platform from which you will launch yourself out of the ordinary limits of perception into a conscious awareness of the spiritual realm.

Begin this initial attunement by retreating to a quiet place where you will not be disturbed. Find a comfortable place to sit and take a minute to relax your body.

Then, bring your attention to bear on what you are experiencing in the present moment. Ignore any distracting thoughts that might arise. Use the ability that you have been practicing to bring your attention fully into your experience of the *now* moment.

Next, begin to imagine that you are allowing your ordinary experience of the moment to gently slip away.

Use your imagination to create a feeling of floating away from your ordinary thoughts and feelings of the moment. This feeling is similar to what you might feel if you are sitting with a group of friends, and someone is telling a story, and your attention begins to drift away. You are ignoring the person telling the story as you begin to float peacefully into a daydream about nothing in particular. The words of the story teller become nothing more than a soft murmur that is occurring in the background of your awareness.

In the same way, in this attunement moment, ignore your own thoughts and create a pleasurable, floating feeling. As this occurs, your ongoing thoughts can slip into the background of your awareness, just as the words of the story teller faded from your attention.

In that moment, your consciousness is beginning to expand beyond the physical reality of where you sit doing your attunement. As that occurs, you are taking the first simple step toward shifting to your Extraordinary Awareness. You are learning to engage the present moment in your *inner* life, and you are leaving the outer physical reality behind.

After you have practiced this simple attunement every day for a week or two, you will be ready for a more focused process that will take you further in the expansion of your awareness. To carry out this second attunement process, it will be necessary to make certain inner preparations. I will describe these preparations briefly now, and then later, I will go into greater depth with them.

Again, start this second attunement by retreating

to a quite place where you will not be disturbed. Then, release the distractions of your physical body. This involves the creation of a deep relaxation, and a strong feeling of *release*. Bodily tension and nervous movements draw your attention to your physical body, which keeps you focused on your ordinary awareness. So, you will create a feeling of releasing all of that so that you can be free of the pressure of your physical sensations on your inner experience.

Next, calm your thoughts and feelings that have to do with the physical world. Because those thoughts and feelings are so strong, when you enter a silent moment of attunement they can overpower your awareness of the moment, making a shift to your second channel of Extraordinary Awareness difficult. Therefore, it is important to calm, smooth over, and then *ignore* those thoughts and feelings.

Then, open your ability to project yourself in your imagination beyond your present limited experience of yourself as a human being. Experiencing yourself in the ordinary human way is like being carried downstream in a river with a strong current. As long as you *desire* to go downstream, then you let the current carry you—as long as you are busy accomplishing in the physical world you allow your attention to be focused on your ordinary awareness.

In this attunement, shifting to your Extraordinary Awareness is like gently lifting yourself out of that strong current so that you can freely and easily move in a different direction. That direction is away from the domination of your ordinary thoughts and feelings, and toward new awarenesses that are related to the spiritual realm.

Following the usual flow of your ordinary awareness in the physical world occurs naturally. It does not take much special attention from you to simply experience your normal thoughts and feelings. The current of your ordinary mental, emotional, and physical habits in the world carries you along.

When you decide to expand your awareness to shift into your Extraordinary Awareness, you are, in a sense, turning in midstream, and at first you may feel that you are struggling to swim upstream against the strong current of ordinary human experience. Turning in midstream does not come as easily as going downstream. However, in time you will discover that once you learn to release your attention from the strong current of ordinary awareness, you will not need to struggle at all. The experience of release will propel you into an effortless inner movement that takes you toward an awareness of the spiritual realm.

Each day, practice this simple attunement process of projecting yourself in your imagination beyond your present limited experience of yourself as a human being. Eventually you will be able to feel that you are releasing yourself from the strong current of ordinary experience. Then, you will be able to create inner experiences that are not dominated by your ordinary thoughts and feelings. You will move toward new experiences that are aligned with your soul in the spiritual realm.

❖

The Sixth Key: Practicing Expanding Your Awareness 117

After you have become familiar with the feeling of not being swept away by your stream of ordinary thoughts and feelings, you can learn to expand your awareness further by using a deeper attunement process. This attunement is accomplished in three steps that will help you continue your inner movement toward awakening to your Extraordinary Awareness.

I suggest that you do this attunement for at least 20 minutes each day. That will prepare you well for the advanced attunement method that you will learn in a later chapter.

Step One. Find a comfortable place to do your attunement where you will not be disturbed. Carry out the relaxation and releasing that you have been practicing in the earlier attunements. Then, you will begin the deepening of your experience by tapping in to the power of your *imagination*. You will do it in the following way.

As you sit in the relaxed silence that you have created, begin to imagine that you are floating upward, out of your ordinary experience. Imagine yourself leaving your ordinary human perceptions behind. You can even imagine that you are floating away from your body and the physical place where you are.

Give yourself time to do this thoroughly, but do it in a completely relaxed and gentle way. Do not try to force your imagining. Let it flow easily, without any effort.

You might imagine visually, seeing a picture of yourself floating away from your physical body. Or, you might simply think about floating, or inwardly feel the sensation. It is not necessary to have actual visual images. You can still begin the process of going beyond your ordinary awareness even if your imagining is vague and involves thoughts or feelings instead of visual images.

By using your imagination in this way, you learn to create new inner experiences that are not dominated by your ordinary thoughts and feelings. Those new experiences will lift you up and carry you effortlessly out of your ordinary experience. With those new experiences, you will be gently floating into an expanded awareness of reality.

This imagining of floating away from your body and your ordinary thoughts and feelings need not be difficult, although you could make it difficult by constantly thinking that it is. It can be quite relaxing and freeing, mentally and emotionally.

However, this imagining alone does not bring on the experience of your soul. It simply begins to free you from the dominance of your ordinary awareness. The second step of this process will help you gain further release from that dominance.

Step Two. You will accomplish this step by using the power of your *will* to create *an elevation of your consciousness beyond imagination*. You will create a *feeling* that takes you beyond what you can imagine.

In your attunement period, once you have spent some time imagining yourself floating away from your physical body, begin to imagine that instead of being your personality self, you are gradually becoming an extraordinary feeling of love. You do not need to create a visual image of this. Instead, use your will to inwardly direct yourself to focus on a powerful feeling of love inside you. If you need help getting the feeling of love started, call forth the feeling of love that you have for a certain person, or even a pet. Create a feeling of the love growing stronger and stronger within you.

Continue to let the love grow until you feel that you are *becoming* the love. Deepen that feeling of being the love. Keep expanding that feeling until you begin to feel that you are a magnificent *being* of love.

Give yourself quite a bit of time to do this. Allow the experience to unfold easily, without any effort. Work with this second step of the process as long as you desire, then go to the third step.

Step Three. In this step, you will gain some momentum in your attunement experience. As you gain that momentum, you will discover something quite amazing. You will discover that in the river of your human awareness, in which the prevailing current of your ordinary thoughts and feelings seems to always be sweeping you into the normal experience of life, there is a subtle *second* current that actually flows away from the physical world toward the spiritual realm of your soul. This is a way of symbolizing your second channel of Extraordinary Awareness.

When you work with this step of awakening to this spiritual current that flows toward expanded awareness, you will eventually realize that there exists in that current an inner *force* that can lift you and help you move along toward the spiritual realm. As you consistently practice this step of your attunement each day, in time, you will feel that you do not need to move the process along as strongly as you did in the beginning. You will feel that expanding your awareness beyond the ordinary is becoming easier. In time, you will experience a powerful force uplifting you in your inner awakening. That force is the guiding influence of your soul.

As this occurs, you will create a more refined awareness within yourself, and the distractions of ordinary awareness will subside enough so that you can begin to align with the more subtle realm of your soul. You will become more sensitive to the inner guidance of your soul. Ultimately, you can become consciously aware of that guidance.

With all of this in mind, you can now accomplish the third step of this process of expansion of consciousness. That step is *to give yourself to the uplifting spiritual force that flows in the river of your awareness. To give yourself to the loving guidance of your own soul.*

As you sit in silence, imagine yourself floating comfortably above the physical world. Feel yourself to be like a soft, white cloud hovering motionless in a clear blue sky. Then, imagine a warm, soft breeze that comes along and begins to gently move you. Without any effort on your part, feel your awareness being carried along by that wonderful breeze.

This kind of imagining will give you the feeling of releasing into the gentle influence and guidance of your soul. By doing this imagining, you allow your soul to draw you strongly into your second channel of Extraordinary Awareness.

You will need to practice this third step for a while to get the feeling of it. It is an inner opening that most people are not used to experiencing. It is so subtle that at first you may think that nothing is happening. In your beginning work with this step, as you try to give yourself to the guidance of your soul, it may seem like you are not receiving anything. Just keep practicing in a gentle, loving way. Eventually, you will be able to release yourself into the wonderful stream of your soul's guidance, and that will carry you toward a beautiful expansion of your awareness. With the gentle help of your soul, you will learn to shift more and more to your Extraordinary Awareness.

These beginning attunements will acquaint you with the creative adjustment of your thoughts, your emotions, and your will that is required to prepare for a deep experience of your soul. The full attunement method that you will learn in a later chapter will be built upon this foundation. The more that you practice these beginning attunements, the stronger your foundation will be for the advanced work that you will do with the full attunement method.

Here, I need to point out that your work to expand your awareness with these beginning attunements can go in fits and starts. Some days you might have a very deep experience and feel that you have made an important breakthrough. Then, the very next day, you might feel heavy, sluggish, and disappointed when you do your attunement. Know that this is normal. Day to day fluctuations in your inner work can be expected.

As you learn to expand your awareness by using attunements in your private inner life, after a while, you can use the experience that you gain in your attunements to shift into an expanded awareness even when you are focused on the outer world. With the harnessing of your attention you can eventually learn to create profound inner experiences even in an ordinary, mundane moment of daily life.

For example, imagine that you are with a friend whom you love very much, and you are talking about the weather. Your awareness is focused on a narrow range of ordinary reality. Yet, in that moment, you can remind yourself that it is possible to expand your awareness of the moment even as your friend is speaking to you. You can do that by creating the same depth of inner experience that you learned to create in your attunements.

First, create the feeling of relaxation and release that you are familiar with from your attunements. Look into your friend's eyes and center your full attention on your friend. Then, carry out the process of expansion of your awareness by using your imagination to begin to trigger the expansion, just as you did in your attunements. Begin to create the feeling of warmth and love that you learned to create in your attunement practice.

Imagine that the love that you have for your friend is a tangible energy that flows between you. You might imagine it as a slight warmth, or a gentle breeze, or a light. Create an imagination of the love energy joining you to your friend.

Next, use your will to create the feeling that you *are* that love, just as you practiced feeling yourself as a being of love in your attunements. In that normally mundane moment, as your friend is speaking to you, become the love that is flowing between yourself and your friend.

Finally, give yourself to the inner guidance of your soul. This guidance will draw you deeper into the experience of being the love that joins you to your friend. By doing this, you can experience your friend in a profound way that goes far beyond what you were able to perceive through your ordinary awareness.

As you practice the process of expanding your awareness in your inner work, and even in the outer world with the people that you love, in time, what you initially set into motion as simply an imagination will eventually become a real and true expanded awareness of a spiritual reality. This can become an awareness of your soul that will gradually build until you are able to consistently perceive the loving presence of your soul during your attunement period. Then, you can even experience such love in your relationships with other people in the outer world.

As you become more sensitive to the influence of your soul in your life, events that you might have dismissed as coincidence will begin to take on a deeper meaning. You will sense that you are inwardly prompted by energies and impulses from your soul to take certain actions, or make certain decisions. What you might have previously thought of as "synchronicity"— the fortuitous coming together of events—can be recognized as a subtle inner guidance from your soul.

That will give you a new perspective on your life. You will begin to understand that every moment of your human life on earth is filled with important purposes that are related to strong guiding impulses from your soul. Such an understanding will bring you deep satisfaction, and it will help you achieve the fulfillment that you desire in your day to day life.

Chapter 10

The Seventh Key: Opening Yourself Emotionally

---- ❋ ----

There is something very important that you need to be aware of as you move on in your work with the twelve keys to higher consciousness. That is, as you open your Extraordinary Awareness to awaken to the spiritual realities of life, you will perceive the spiritual realm through your *intuition*.

Then, you will need to understand that your intuition is intimately woven with your *emotions*. Therefore, if you tighten your emotions, you will tighten your intuition, and that will block your ability to directly experience your soul and the spiritual realm. When you understand this, you can see why the seventh key to higher consciousness is: *Opening yourself emotionally*.

On your path of enlightenment, the process of expanding your awareness involves working creatively with the important and dominant aspect of your personality self that is your *emotional* life. If you close down your feelings and thereby suppress your intuitive abilities, that will make it difficult for you to awaken to an experience of your soul. When you open emotionally, you stimulate your intuition, making it easier to intuitively sense and feel the loving influence of your soul in your life.

Before we look at ways to open emotionally, I want to give you a view of human emotions that has inspired me in my own inner work. This goes beyond the traditional psychological understanding of emotions.

Begin with the thought that there is an amazing uniqueness in *your personal feelings*. This is due to the fact that *your* emotions are a private subjective experience that can occur *only* inside *you*. In other words, your emotions cannot occur inside any other living being, in the direct sense. Other people might have similar feelings inside themselves, but *your* feelings cannot occur anywhere except *inside your human experience*.

This means that the "mechanism" of your personal emotions lives only in your human self. Therefore, your particular emotions as they occur inside you are *a unique reality*. In all of life, in all of the realms, there are no other realities that are *your personal emotions*.

That uniqueness tells you that something quite miraculous has occurred in order to make it possible for your subjective feelings to be "one-of-a-kind" in all of reality. The miraculous fact that you have your unique feelings is attributable to your soul. Your soul created your human self and gave that human self the ability to have feelings that no other being can have. Your emotional capacity is a divine gift from your soul.

From my extensive research into the spiritual realm, I have come to view the human feeling capacity as an aspect of divine energies. We are able to have feelings because of certain spiritual energies that our soul has placed into our personality self energy structure. In addition to enabling us to have feelings, those spiritual energies also give us the capacity for thinking, remembering, imagining, conceptualizing, and all of the other inner abilities that make our life so rich.

Thinking about your emotions as a divine gift naturally raises the question: How did *negative* feelings come about?

I believe that in the beginning of human life on earth, emotions were experienced in a pure way. People continually felt the human love that joined them together. They felt the divine love that constantly poured into them from the souls. There were no negative feelings. There was no subjective experience of emotional pain.

Also, people were clearly aware that *they were not their feelings*. They experienced themselves as wonderful humans who were *having* feelings, not *being* those feelings. They were also well aware that *all feelings are temporary*.

In that early stage of human life, the ability to have emotions was clearly experienced as a divine gift from the souls that was woven into the human personality self energy structures and aligned with the physical bodies in a loose manner. Without the burden of negative feelings, living humans could remain aware of the truth that *the souls' purpose for life on earth was for humans to create joy and love, and for them to feel the magnificence of eternal perfection while alive in a physical body through their ability to have emotions.* Therefore, at that time, due to the divinely-given ability to *feel*, people were able to have pure emotional experiences of divine love.

Through the ages, as humans exercised their free will, they began to make personal choices that were *not* rooted in divine love and perfection. Those were choices that led to the manifestation of self-preoccupation and selfishness. As the selfishness grew, negative human behaviors came about. Those behaviors caused humans to respond with negative feelings. Where before they were no negative feelings, now there was disappointment, frustration, sadness, despair, and the other negative emotions that we are all so familiar with in our present lives.

We all have been given the divine gift of emotions. Now, thanks to the confused use of human free will through the ages, we also have the *human* "gift" of negative feelings. Yet, the unique emotional experiences that you have within you are still part of the mystical interaction between your human self and your soul. The true nature of life, if put into words, could be described as *an ongoing, eternal experience of goodness* that can be perceived from *different levels*. You, as a *soul*, are perceiving that ongoing eternal experience of goodness from the spiritual realm. You, as a *human*, due to your ability to *feel* that has been placed into you by your soul, can learn to experience that goodness as an individual self living within a physical body on the earth.

Early on in my own spiritual quest, when I took a completely intellectual approach to life and was not open emotionally, I believed that spiritual realities are perceived by the mind through thoughts. I did not realize that they are perceived intuitively by the heart through feelings.

You will not use your mind to perceive the spiritual realm. You will use your feelings, your sensing, your intuition to experience the spiritual realm. Then, you can use your mind to process the experience after the fact.

If you are emotionally tight, if you have closed your feelings to avoid emotional pain, you will need to do some inner work to encourage yourself to make an emotional opening. You can begin by simply paying more attention to all of your feelings. Notice what you are feeling throughout the day. Encourage yourself to make your feelings important. Explore them and experience them fully whenever you can.

You can say this affirmation to yourself as a statement of purpose in your movement toward more emotional openness:

> "To fully bring forth my intuitive ability to experience my soul, I will move toward more emotional openness. I will encour-

> age myself to *feel* deeply in all areas of my life. Every day, I will explore the entire range of human emotions freely, without resistance."

The reason that we do not have a full emotional openness all the time is that we all have a dislike of emotional pain. We are afraid that if we live each day being entirely open and emotionally vulnerable, people will take advantage of us, or they will not treat us well, and we will have a lot of negative, painful feelings. To avoid that, we all tend to hold back our feelings at times.

People do that to differing degrees. Some people are not open with anyone. Others will only be open to people that they trust and love. And some will tend to be open and warm with everyone that they know.

Emotional openness and vulnerability can come about when we are willing to release our fears of being hurt emotionally. If we do not release those fears, then they will tend to dominate our interactions with other people, they will negatively color our responses to life, and they will cause us to be emotionally protected, rather that emotionally open. (In the next chapter I will show you how to release fears and negative feelings that stand in the way of emotional openness.)

When you are interacting with other people, you can choose to ignore any feelings of fear or negativity that you might carry inside you, and you can *will* yourself to be open emotionally. You can do that even when there might be some potential emotional pain, as long as the situation is not physically threatening to you. Usually, that leads to results in your life that will be more satisfying than results that you achieve when you are being emotionally protected and closed.

For example, imagine that you are in a romantic relationship with someone that you love deeply. However, that person has another lover. It would be normal for you to be afraid that you might be rejected for the other lover, which would be very painful. So, you decide to be emotionally distant in the relationship and you hold back from expressing your love to the person. You decide: "I will protect myself, I will not feel deeply. That way I can avoid some emotional pain." As a result of that choice, you are cold and aloof to your loved one. Because you are so unemotional, your loved one grows less interested in you and eventually you are rejected for the other lover.

Imagining a different scenario, you could say: "I am frightened that if I love this person deeply, this one will love someone else and reject me, and it will be too painful. But, when I am communicating with this person that I love, *I will ignore my fear*. I will choose to be sensitive and emotionally open. I will feel my love for this person and I will express it fully. If the result of that happens to be a rejection and some emotional pain, so be it. I refuse to live my life in fear of emotional pain. I am determined to be as emotionally open as I can in loving this person."

If you are not one of those rare people who is always emotionally open with everyone, then you may need to *will* yourself to be more open. You will need to make an ongoing commitment to being as emotionally open as you can in all of your relationships. In those relationships you will need to continually practice creating more emotional openness.

You can think of the process of opening emotionally in terms of four focal points. By working with these you can move forward in your opening.

Focal Point One: Challenge Yourself. Constantly challenge yourself to go beyond familiar emotions. As you have the same feelings that you are used to having in your relationships, and about life, first *accept* your familiar emotions and appreciate them fully. Then, say to yourself: "*There is more.*" Stimulate yourself to go beyond the familiar feelings. Creatively nudge yourself to feel more, to invite stronger feelings, to invite new feelings. Train yourself to create more in the emotional area.

Focal Point Two: Create New Contexts. Be alert for ways to establish a *context* outside of what you are familiar with in order to stimulate new, expanded feelings that are not dominated by old habits of emotional tightness. For example, imagine that in a certain relationship with a friend you always behave and communicate in the same way that does not stir up any particularly deep feelings. That would be your *normal* context.

To expand your feelings, you could create some new contexts in your relationship with your friend. You could try meeting your friend in new, interesting places. You could do new, satisfying activities together. That would create a new context that would help you have some new, expanded feelings to share with your friend. Often, stepping outside of your familiar experiences can help you create new emotional responses to other people, and to your life.

Focal Point Three: Open More to Other People. You can think of yourself as needing "cross pollination" from other people. If you always focus on your own thoughts, ideas, and feelings in your relationships with others, you will not be open to being stimulated by their different ways of thinking, feeling, and viewing life. If you pay more attention to other people and become more interested in them, you will be able to have new experiences that can lead you to create new feelings.

Some people who do not have many relationships, or who have trouble deepening their feelings in the relationships that they already have, may need to concentrate on meeting new people. That would be an effective way to invite more cross-pollination from others.

Focal Point Four: Go Beyond Human Limitations. Each day, after you have done everything that you can think of to be as emotionally open as you can be in the normal human sense, then you can take a few minutes at the end of the day to sit quietly and invite your feelings to expand in a way that will include feelings about your spiritual existence as a soul. That can help you create feelings that go beyond the limits of human emotions.

You can use these words to begin to stimulate your emotions to expand toward feelings that are related to your soul:

> "I now release all of my emotional tightness and human limitations. I become receptive to stimulations from my soul to move me toward expanded feelings about life. I am a vessel into which my soul can now pour wonderful feelings. I invite my soul to fill me with expanded emotions that will help me feel the true beauty of life."

Another way to expand your emotional life is to become aware of how your emotions are manipulated by events in your life in the outer world, and then create feelings based on what you desire, rather than on what you believe the world if forcing upon you. As you learn to do that, you can create new, expanded feelings that will bring you more joy.

Everyone seems to have difficulty going beyond the normal responses to the outside world. We can all feel: "If someone treats me well then I will feel good. If someone mistreats me then I will feel bad." What this means is that we tend to believe that we are *made* to feel good or bad by other people. I consider this to be the lowest level of insight, and it is rooted in self-preoccupation.

I believe that the highest level of understanding is when we honestly live through whatever feelings are stirred up in us by other people and events in the world, then me remember that we can go beyond those feelings. We can create new feelings.

We can also remember that the feelings that we are having in any moment about our life in the world are "realities" that are occurring only in our private subjective experience. We can tend to become preoccupied with our private experience and continue to focus only on ourselves, which will cause us to miss what other people are experiencing in that moment. If we did that, then our emotions would be limited by our self-preoccupation. On the other hand, we could turn our attention to other people and that would open the way for expanding our feelings beyond our own limited experience.

Emotional sensitivity to others expands our emotional life, while self-preoccupation tends to contract it. When you spend time paying attention to other people, you are more likely to be sensitive, kind, and compassionate. Those are expanded feelings that you would not usually create if you were only focused on yourself.

Seen from this point of view, you might say that the best way to squeeze your emotional life is to be continually self-preoccupied and focus *only* on yourself. The best way to expand your emotions is to extend yourself and pay more attention to the people in your life. Through sincere, honest communication with other people you can accelerate your expansion of your emotional life.

The greatest emotional opening occurs when we are willing to create feelings of kindness, compassion, and love for other people. However, most people are not willing to create such feelings unless other people please them and treat them well. We all tend to wait for the other person to give to us first, then we are willing to respond with strong positive feelings. It is almost as if we feel that people have to earn our positive feelings before we give them. And certainly we do not want to give kindness, compassion, and love to people that displease us or mistreat us. Those people do not "deserve" it.

We are all involved in a process of breaking this shell of too much self-preoccupation. We are gaining knowledge and experience that can help us refine our emotional life by adding sensitivity to other people to our intense concern for our own thoughts, feelings, desires, and all that we focus upon in ourselves day after day. We are learning to make wise, creative choices about our feelings that can take us out of too much self-preoccupation and can lead to expanded feelings in all areas of our lives.

This does not mean that you will ignore your desires for your own personal fulfillment. It means that you will use your intelligence to integrate your own desires with kindness, compassion, and love toward other people.

With practice you can monitor your feelings and make choices that do not squeeze your feelings out of fear. You can learn to orchestrate your feelings in ways that you believe are best in each moment. When you see an opportunity for expanding your feelings by opening to other people, you can choose to do that.

❖

Another effective way to expand your emotions is to learn to create feelings of *goodness* within yourself. Clearly, there are many differences among people in terms of what they think, and feel, and believe, as well as how they choose to act in the world. Yet, in every human there is *the same desire to create goodness for themselves that you have within you.* The only difference between humans is what each individual believes goodness to be.

If a person is a glutton, then to them goodness is eating a great deal of food in order to experience the strong sensual pleasure of eating. For a finely trained athlete, goodness could be eating a moderate amount of food, not for the pleasure of it, but for the intelligent choice of nutrients to make their body strong. These two individuals would have entirely different beliefs about what makes goodness.

For many people, goodness is the satisfying of their strong sensual appetites and desires, in terms of personal pleasure. So, you could say that at the lower "animal" level, the human sense of goodness is entirely caught up in the feeling: "I desire this for my own sensual pleasure."

In the higher expression of goodness, a person will consider the long-term results of their choices in their attempt to achieve goodness for themselves. They will also consider other people.

Often, the animal level will overpower people, particularly in the sexual area. As a generalization, many people will have the feeling: "I *must* have my sexual pleasure. I will not be so concerned with the feelings of my sexual partners. What really matters is my pleasure."

At the higher level, individuals would integrate a concern for other people into their own seeking of sexual pleasure. Usually, that will draw in the experience of *love* into the sexual expression.

You can examine your own life to see if there are any negative consequences of acting on your own personal desires for goodness when you are not considering the wellbeing of other people. It is not that you would need to condemn yourself for that approach, but simply be aware that, symbolically speaking, you are functioning at the animal level. And, generally, that will create more challenges in your relationships with other people.

Then, on the other side, you can observe the impact of choices that you make to achieve what you consider to be goodness when those choices are integrated with a concern for other people. In that expression, you step out of the entirely self-involved animal expression, and you rise to a higher level where the actions that you take to fulfill your desires are woven with a sensitivity to other people. The impact of those higher level choices will usually be more harmony and more goodness for everyone concerned. Those kinds of experiences will encourage you to continue to open emotionally.

You can observe the choices that you make each day and you can decide for yourself what is the best way to orchestrate your emotional life. However, as you move along on your path of enlightenment, you will learn that when you create feelings of goodness for yourself, in alignment with a willingness to expand your feelings of goodness towards others, that will be the quickest way to achieve more meaningful experiences in life.

To summarize these important points, I will say that one of the best methods for encouraging emotional openness is to pay more attention to giving to other people. When you give to other people you transcend the human self-preoccupation that envelops us all. Through that giving, you stimulate an emotional opening within you that becomes a bridge between yourself as you live within your private reality, and all that exists outside of your subjective experience. You invite the experience and the love of other people into your life, and that can stimulate you and help you expand and deepen your emotions.

In your work to open to other people, you will want to balance the attention that you give to yourself against the attention that you give to the people in your life. A good way to monitor yourself each day is to use the image of a balance scale with a pan on each side. At the end of each day, imagine that all of the attention that you have focused on yourself is placed onto one side of the balance. See it pulling down that side of the scale. If you did not give your attention to anybody else that day, your scale would be way out of balance. If you paid attention to others and gave to them, there would be something on the other side of the scale to balance it out. Each day you can check this balance and decide if you want to make any changes in it.

We all tend to pay more attention to ourselves in a typical day that we do to other people. But, this image of the scale will at least help you see when you are totally caught up with yourself and not giving at all to other people. For the rare people who are *constantly* giving to others, this will help them become aware that they are out of balance in the other direction, and they will realize that they need to give more to themselves.

❖

To help maintain a healthy balance between yourself and others, you can also think in terms of *attention energies* flowing *into* you, and those energies flowing *out* of you. When you are giving your attention to yourself, you can imagine that your own energies are flowing into you. That is a taking in of your own energy of attention. When you are giving to others, you can imagine your attention energy flowing out of you. Thinking in this way, at the end of each day, you can assess what the balance was between taking in and flowing out.

No matter how wonderful it is to pay attention to yourself, if that is *all* that you do, then you will only take in your energy and you will become "overstuffed," or blocked. Your human energies in your personality can temporarily become unbalanced toward the *self*. That can result in selfishness, and the creation of a gap between yourself and other people.

When you give to other people, you begin the outpouring of your energies of caring, compassion, and loving. Such an outpouring creates experiences that are very important for your emotional life. They can broaden and expand your human feelings, stimulating deeper love and fulfillment within you. Also, other people benefit a great deal from what you give to them. Seeing them benefit from your giving can bring great joy into your life, and that experience will prompt deeper emotional openings within you.

It would be quite unusual, and perhaps even impossible, for you to live every moment of your life *perfectly* balanced between giving your attention energies to yourself and to other people. It is simply not in our human nature to be that uniform, or that perfect. Human nature is volatile and robust. You might say that it is "experimental." So, to guide yourself in your balance between taking for yourself and giving to others, you can think in terms of making *continual adjustments* every day, instead of trying to establish a perfect, permanent balance.

In this process of continual adjustment, *you* are the one who must decide each day what you need to do in order to create the best balance—whether to adjust the balance by giving more attention to yourself, or whether to lean toward more attention given to others.

When you decide that it is good to focus your attention on others and give to them, *you* will decide what you will give, to whom, when, where, and how. As you make those decisions, it is wise to balance *what you desire to give*, with *what others need to receive*. So, it is always wise to ask people: "What do you need? How can I help you?"

In my experience I have found that most people need to receive compassion, warmth, encouragement, and love from others. In almost every moment of your life, the people around you will deeply need those gifts from you. If you are willing to give them, not only will others benefit, but you will be opening emotionally through giving.

The gentle emotional openings that you make when you try to care more about others, when you give to them, and when you are kind and generous to them, will *soften* your own personality. When you soften, you create more thoughts and feelings that are positive, creative, and more aligned with the true spiritual energies of life. By becoming softer through your willingness to try to be kind, sensitive, and generous to others, you will create a strong, positive, and beneficial reflective action back into your own personality self patterns. That will stimulate those patterns toward growth and fulfillment.

Through time, the stimulation of those patterns will bring about more and more emotional opening within you. That emotional opening will stimulate your intuitive abilities that are woven with your emotions. The awakening of your intuitive abilities will then enable you to use them more often to become aware of the loving presence of your soul. Such experiences accumulated year after year become the inner power that moves you along on your joyful path of enlightenment.

Chapter 11

The Eighth Key: Transforming Your Negative Feelings

---- ※ ----

You are gaining a deeper understanding of what is involved in using your Extraordinary Awareness to attain a direct experience of your soul and the spiritual realm. To continue building toward a more enlightened experience, you can now begin to work with the eighth key to higher consciousness. This powerful key is: *The transformation of your negative feelings.*

Since your feelings dramatically affect everything that you do in your life, you will need to have a clear understanding of your various emotional patterns so that you can discover and transform any habits of negative feeling that you might have. If you expand your emotional life without transforming those negative patterns, then as you begin to have new, expanded experiences that go beyond your ordinary human reality, those new experiences can be distorted by your negative emotional patterns.

It is quite normal and expected that everyone will have negative feelings at times. However, you do not need to allow those feelings to dominate your daily experience of life. You are not a slave to your feelings. When your negative feelings come up, you can work with them creatively in order to transform them. That will open the way for a full and clear expansion of your awareness. Your negative feelings will not stand in the way of your awakening to your soul. You will learn to have experiences of your soul that are not blocked, or distorted by any negative feelings that you might create.

If you do not work consistently to transform your strong negative feelings, over time, they can build up a "pressure" inside you. Then, when you are trying to expand into a higher awareness, that negative pressure will prevent you from feeling enough trust and love to be able to inwardly release and fully open yourself.

Learning to transform negative feelings is a very important aspect of the enlightenment process, particularly for people who do not have a great deal of harmony in their lives. They might be struggling with poor health, or a lack of money, or a challenging and painful relationship. They might be desperately lonely because they do not have any love in their life. Perhaps they are depressed because they feel that they have no important purpose in life. Such people can work with their *outer* circumstances to try to change them and create more of what will please them and make them happy. However, there are times when those circumstances cannot be changed. In such cases, in order to create happiness in the face of ongoing challenges in the outside world, a person will need to discover the great power that we all have within us to change and master our own negative feelings.

We always have that power to change our feelings, but many people do not believe it because they feel so bad about their life. Since they cannot *feel* that power, they do not know that they have it. So, they unintentionally allow their negative feelings to go on in ever-increasing spirals through the years.

We all dislike feeling bad. We want to eliminate painful feelings as soon as we can. But, if you develop a dread of experiencing your negative feelings, not only will that make you unhappy, but it will block the opening of your Extraordinary Awareness.

Given the many negative things in the world, such as poverty, illness, crime, war, disease, and so many other terrible circumstances, and all of the information about those negative events that is fed to us daily through the media, it is not surprising that we have become adept at creating negative feelings. Since it appears that there are so many things in the world that are deadly, that can destroy us, we can create an ongoing sense of *badness* about life.

Certainly, it is a fact that circumstances in the

physical world can destroy your physical body. Sooner or later, something will cause the death of your body. However, as you discover how to awaken your Extraordinary Awareness, you will begin to understand that nothing can destroy your *being*. You are an eternal soul. You have lived many lifetimes on earth. Every one of those lives has ended in death. But, *you* have never died.

The sense of badness that you create about the real threats in the world will naturally spill over into your feelings about aspects of life that are *not* particularly threatening. You can unintentionally infuse into your experience of daily life an exaggerated sense of fear about something terrible happening, even when you are having "non-lethal" challenges. For example, if you believe that you are not wealthy enough to please you, or if you feel that you are not loved perfectly enough by other people, or if you believe that the home that you live in is not quite perfect enough, then you might create a feeling that you will never be happy, that you will always be miserable, and your life will be ruined. You can feel that such displeasing circumstances will cause an extreme badness that will never go away.

Faced with such strong, ongoing negative feelings, over time, many people can become depressed. Then they can begin to feel that such bad emotions are so terrible that they cannot stand them. They become afraid of having their strong negative feelings. Under the influence of that fear, they might try to force themselves to have positive thoughts and feelings in order to make their bad feelings go away. Or, they might distract themselves from the bad feelings with pleasurable experiences in the physical world, particularly strong sensual pleasures such as food, sex, alcohol, or even drugs. In that way they continue to avoid their negative feelings, but, as a consequence, they also continue *to deepen their fear of having the negative feelings.*

Although such distractions may temporarily help people ignore their negative feelings, they do not heal the feelings. Then, as they continue to ignore their negative feelings, they can create a generalized *fear of badness*. It could be a dread of something that they cannot clearly define. They may not be able to say specifically why they feel frightened. They will simply feel a terrible, pervasive badness, and they will feel that they must eliminate that disturbing feeling at all costs.

If you fearfully try to avoid experiencing your negative feelings by forcefully pushing yourself toward positive thoughts and feelings, or by distracting yourself with strong activities in the outer world, that might help you feel better in the moment. However, over time, that will lead to a *greater* fear of having negative feelings.

The consistent creation of feelings of badness can bring about a constant, exaggerated sense of *seriousness* about life, and a feeling of ongoing anxiety about not being able to be happy or successful. You can go around with a nagging, underlying feeling that something terrible will happen to you if you do not achieve what you believe will make you happy in life. It is as if you are playing a game, and you believe that if you lose the game the penalty is *death*. In such a game you would play with desperation and fear. You would play a very *serious* game. On the other hand, if you knew that the only penalty for losing the game would be that you would feel bad for a while because you lost, then you would play the game with a sense of freedom, and even *enjoyment*—which is the purpose for playing the game.

You can often create a very serious, negative feeling about life, even when your challenges are not that great in the immediate moment. You can create negative feelings that can actually make your life miserable if you allow them to control you year after year. What you need to learn is that *you can control your feelings*, rather than allowing them to control you.

When you do have some serious challenges in your life, such as poverty, or illness, or desperate loneliness, then naturally you will feel bad. However, even with such challenges, you have an ability to fully experience the negative feelings that you have about your challenges, and then you can learn to transform those negative feelings. You do not need to feel that *life* is terrible and full of badness because you have some negative feelings about your challenges.

If you can change the challenges in your life in the outside world that cause you to feel bad, then your negative feelings will usually go away for a while. However, when you cannot change the challenging situations, you can still change *the feelings of badness* that you have created about those challenges. You do not need to spend endless days feeling that life on earth is bad. No matter what stimulates your feelings of badness about life, you can live through those feelings, and you can learn to release them, even if the outside world does not change to perfectly please you.

Your negative feelings can be stimulated by many different things, such as difficult, painful situations in your life. They can be stirred up by information that you have absorbed from the media about terrible things going on in the world. They might even be strong negative feelings that you have from painful memories of your childhood. Your negative inner experiences can be stirred up by almost anything that you do not like in the world. It could be something quite small and simply irritating, or it could be something that is dramatically negative.

For example, you might be a person who feels bad about life because you hate violence and war, and you are feeling depressed because there is so much of it in the world. In that situation, you could feel that you can never be happy until violence and war end. If you did create such an attitude, you would have a great struggle in trying to feel happy because it appears that violence and war may not end in our lifetime.

In this example, you do not have the power to make yourself happy by going out and stopping violence and war in the outside world. But, you do have the power to work with your inner experience to transform your negative feelings, and that would open the way for you to achieve happiness even if violence and war continue to occur in the world.

You have the power to change your feelings of

badness, even if the world does not change to please you and make you happy. You can heal your negative feelings, and you can create new, positive ones. Even in a world that has much human-created negativity, you do have the power to fairly consistently create feelings that inspire you and that help you to feel more joy and goodness in life.

Clearly, there are differing degrees in the seriousness of the causes of negative feelings. And, the intensity of the negative feelings will usually be directly proportional to the degree of perceived negativity in the event. Being irritated with a friend would be perceived by most people as a minor negativity, and they would not likely respond to that particular event with unusually strong negative feelings. But, in the extreme seriousness of war, for example, most people would respond with extreme negativity—extremely negative feelings.

What you will learn on your path of enlightenment is that no matter what experience in the outer world may have caused your negative feelings, once the negative experience had ended and is no longer directly affecting you, then your remaining challenge will be *the feelings of badness* that you are creating in the present moment. And, you can learn to stop creating those feelings.

To begin to work creatively with your negative feelings you need to understand that they are not *truths* about you or your life. You will never be free if you accept your negative feelings as truths. If they were truths, then they would be permanent. You would not be able to do anything to change them. You would be stuck with them for life. Your freedom lies in accepting your negative feelings as temporary human experiences. If they are temporary, then they can be changed.

You create your negative thoughts and feelings because of underlying *fears* in your human personality self. Those fears could be caused by anything in your present life, or even by patterns that you have brought forward from a past lifetime. Whatever might cause your fears, when you have them they create a temporary loss of confidence in the goodness of life.

Many people think of fear as only a feeling of *fright*. But, fear can also be understood as *any bad feeling inside you*. For most people, when they are having a feeling of badness of any kind, it is usually a fear that is not so clearly defined. It can be a vague feeling of: "Something will damage me. Something will destroy me." It can be any feeling that makes you believe that there is badness in your life. It is a feeling that *goodness* is not present in that moment. Healing your fear, and transforming your negative feelings, involves a process of regaining your trust that there *is* goodness in your life, and in the world.

Imagine that you come into a room full of people. That room and those people represent your daily life in the outer world. If you believe that your mortal enemy is in that room waiting to kill you, you will naturally feel a great deal of fear. You certainly will not feel safe in that room.

If you come into the very same room expecting to

meet a dear friend whom you have not seen for a long time, your mindset and emotions will be very positive. That is because there will be no fear.

It is the same with your human life. When you heal your fearful feelings, you can enter the "room" of human life as if you are meeting a dear friend. You can trust that there is goodness in life.

As you work to transform your negative feelings that grow out of your fear, it is important to know that no matter what it is in the outside world that stirs up your various negative feelings, those feelings all have something in common. They are all taking place *inside you*. This means that they can all be transformed by working with your own subjective experience. You do not need to change the outside world to make your negative feelings go away. You only need to change your negative experiences inside you where the negative feelings are happening.

Most people do not change their negative feelings naturally because our innate animal instinct tends to drive us away from anything that is painful. So, when our negative feelings come up, our first impulse is to run away from them. However, as I have pointed out, the more that we try to avoid our negative feelings, the more frightening they become. If you try to force your negative feelings to go away, you will simply create a stronger fear of having those feelings.

People who continually run away from their negative feelings and become more afraid of experiencing them usually spend a lot of time obsessing about negative feelings. They might spend years looking for psychological explanations for *why* they have negative feelings. That is done in an attempt to make those feelings go away. That process, which is rooted in a fear of having the feelings, prevents them from coming to the realization that the real reason that they continue to have consistent negative feelings is that they have not practiced healing their fears. They have not practiced working with negative feelings when they have them in order to learn to fully experience them, live through them, and then release them.

Instead of running away from your negative feelings, you can use the following simple, but effective method for transforming them. I have used this process successfully in my own life, and it has helped many of my students to transform their negative feelings. This method is for the *normal* range of everyday negative feelings, not for exaggerated psychological problems.

The method for transforming your negative feelings is not difficult to understand. However, it may require some practice over a period of time to fully master it. It is carried out in three stages. I call them: (1) the "wallowing" in the negative feelings stage; (2) the releasing stage; and, (3) the returning to the truth stage.

Stage One: Wallowing in the Feelings. The process of transforming your negative feelings—from the smallest negative feelings to the largest—begins with your willingness to *completely experience* those feelings. You will need to have the courage to fully engage any dark, fearful, or depressing feelings that you have created, whenever they arise, without trying to immediately make those feelings go away.

Begin to do this by finding a private place, sit quietly, and close your eyes. Then, take ten minutes to fully *accept* and *experience* any negative feelings that you want to work with. Just let them happen. Feel them intensely without any resistance. Try to experience them as deeply as possible. You can even exaggerate them. Make the negative feelings as strong as you can so that you can fully experience their intensity. There is no need to do this for more than ten minutes.

At first, you might find it troubling to sit and fully feel your negative feelings for ten minutes. However, in time, you will discover that this step of the process will be very freeing. You will learn that you do not need to run away from your own negative feelings. You can stand your ground, and you can say: "I am having some challenging emotions. So be it. Let me get on with it and live through the feelings."

Doing this first step of the transformation process will eventually teach you that no matter how painful your negative feelings might be during this ten minute period, *they will not damage your being*. The "frightened child" inside you will be comforted and reassured that it is not in danger simply because there are some negative feelings being experienced.

As you successfully carry out this "wallowing" in the negative feelings stage of the transformation process, you will realize that you are receiving a great deal of benefit from it. The greatest benefit will be that *you will have trained yourself not to be afraid of your own negative feelings*.

In working with this stage of the process, if you find yourself becoming deeply disturbed, or unusually depressed, then stop doing the process for a while. Wait for a few days until you feel stronger and try it again. If you continue to feel your negative feelings so strongly that you are afraid to go on with the work, you might need a friend or a loved one to do the process with you. If this process continues to stir up too much fear, either stop doing it altogether, or perhaps find a psychological professional to help you work through your negative feelings.

Stage Two: Releasing the Feelings. For some people the releasing stage of the transformation process can seem difficult at first. When you have just intensely experienced some strong negative feelings, you might not expect to be able to immediately release those feelings. However, with practice you can learn to do that.

As you work more and more with the cycles of creating the negative feelings, then fully experiencing them for ten minutes, and then releasing them, you will discover that your feelings are *flexible* and *changeable*. You will learn to go *into* your feelings and *out of* them at will. You will discover that you do not need to allow your feelings to dominate you. You will awaken to the fact that you have the inner power to master your feelings.

Most people do not realize that they have that power over their feelings. They allow the events and circumstances of their life to toss their feelings about.

If something occurs that they do not like, then they always feel bad. If something occurs that they like, then they feel happy. They usually spend their lives hoping that something that they like will always occur so that they can feel happy all the time, and hoping that something that they do not like will never occur so that they do not need to feel bad.

Your feelings will always be impacted by circumstances in your life. When those circumstances are negative, you will usually feel bad. However, by practicing the transformation process, you will reduce the amount of time that you spend feeling bad about your negative emotions.

After you have completed the "wallowing" stage of the transformation process, you are ready to move to *releasing* the negative feelings that you have just fully experienced. You can begin the releasing stage by saying this affirmation to yourself:

> "**My feelings of badness are *temporary* experiences. I have just lived through these negative feelings and they have not harmed me. They will *never* harm me. These feelings have not changed the inner goodness within my human self. I am still the same wonderful person that I was before I had these negative feelings.**
>
> **I now call upon the inner power that I have to master my feelings and I begin to create a feeling of relaxation. I am creating a feeling of *releasing* the feelings of negativity that I have just lived through.**"

This stage of releasing your negative feelings involves *a felt emotional shift* that you will learn to create inside you. You can use some thoughts to set that shift into motion, then it is something that you will eventually be able to create and *feel* in your inner experience. It is sensation of going from an experience of darkness or dread, into a sudden feeling of release from the darkness that you have been enveloped in. It is as if the darkness is dissolving into a new feeling of freedom from all burdens, and a feeling of entering lightness, comfort, peace, and tranquility.

To try to help people sense what this elusive feeling of release is like, I often use the idea of having a dramatically negative situation suddenly reversed. For example, imagine that a person that you deeply love is scheduled to take a trip on a plane. You know the exact flight that they will be on. As you sit at home watching television, you see a special news bulletin that reports that the flight that your loved one is on has crashed and everyone aboard was killed. You can understand that in that moment you would be swallowed up in intense feelings of badness. Then, imagine that your phone rings, you answer it, and it is your loved one saying that they missed the flight that crashed. Immediately, you have a feeling of *release* from the badness that had swallowed you. That is the kind of felt emotional shift that you will learn to make as you work with the releasing stage of the process of transforming your negative feelings.

If you want to use your *thoughts* to set the felt emotional shift into motion, you can use the following affirmation as you begin the releasing of your negative feelings:

> **"My feelings of negativity are now dissolving. They were only a temporary dark cloud. That cloud is now being swept away by a sweet, fresh inner breeze of goodness that is now flowing through me. I feel the tightness and heaviness of those negative feelings being carried away from me. I am beginning to feel a delicious relaxation coming over me. I am now entering a wonderful and comforting feeling of peace and tranquility."**

Imagine this, or think this as strongly as you can. That will help you begin to create the actual *feeling* of release. Then, sit quietly and continue to invite a feeling of relaxation and peace. Allow that to comfort you as you create the inner shift from the previous negative feelings to the feelings of peacefulness. Continue to allow the feeling of peacefulness to grow within your inner experience.

Stage Three: Returning to the Truth. After taking as much time as you need in the releasing stage, then you can move on to the third stage of the transformation process, which is *the return to truth*. In the state of relaxation that you have created in your feelings during the releasing stage, you can draw upon the power of your mind to begin to think the truth about you, and about life.

This stage will require you to think the "highest" thoughts that you can, which means that your thoughts

The Eighth Key: Transforming Your Negative Feelings 159

need to be of a beautiful, spiritual nature. They need to be thoughts that have nothing to do with the complexity of your human life. You have just released your negative feelings about your life on earth, now it is time to create an inner experience based upon what you believe to be the highest truth about life—your highest ideals.

If you are confused about the truth about yourself and about life, or, if you do not have any particularly strong spiritual ideals and beliefs, then you can use the following suggestions and focal points. These are the kinds of thoughts that I have used successfully in my own work with the transformation process.

To begin this stage of turning your attention to the truth, take a few deep breaths and invite a deepening of the feeling of relaxation and tranquility that you have been creating in the previous stage. Then, initiate your thoughts about the truth of your human experience, and your existence as a soul, by using these words:

> **"The negative feelings that I have just lived through were *temporary* experiences inside me. I have lived through the worst of them, and I have released them. The *truth* is that those negative feelings *did not harm my being*."**

Then, you can reinforce this truth by saying to yourself:

> **"*All* of my negative feelings are temporary. They can *never* damage my being."**

Then, it can be beneficial to remind yourself of the truth of your larger existence beyond the physical world. You can do that by saying the following words to yourself:

> **"The truth is that I am a wonderful human being, and, I am a magnificent eternal soul. There is a loving goodness that permeates all of life. That divine loving goodness is filling me in this moment, and in all moments of my life."**

Remember that even the most horrible negative feelings that you might experience cannot diminish the loving goodness of life.

Another truth to remind yourself of is: Negative feelings do not change the purpose of human life on earth. That purpose is not for us to learn through challenges and emotional pain, as many people believe. The *true* purpose of life on earth is to experience the goodness and love that our souls continually experience in the spiritual realm. To remind yourself of this truth, you can use these words:

> **"My human life on earth is intended to be a wonderful, joyful *play*ground, not a dark, frightening *battle*ground. The true purpose of life on earth is *joy*, and *laughter*, and *happiness*, and *love*. In this moment, I am aligning with that purpose, and I am creating feelings of joy, and happiness, and love inside me."**

You have the human power that has been given to you by your soul to *think* and to *feel*. You continually use that power to *create* your own inner experience. Usually, you do that day after day without noticing what you are actually creating. Like everyone, you allow circumstances to trigger negative feelings inside you, and then you do not notice that you continue to create those feelings.

If you continue to create negative feelings without learning to release them, you will not feel the power that you have within you to create feelings of goodness, and, you can feel helpless in the face of the negative events of the world. That is the human "battleground"—working with the inner power that you inadvertently and unintentionally use to create negative feelings inside you, and a lack of knowledge about ways to use your power to create joy, harmony, and love.

As you sit silently in this stage of the transformation process of returning to the truth, use that power to create a moment of *goodness* for yourself inside your unique subjective reality. Create feelings of beauty, harmony, majesty, love, and goodness of any kind. Feel the power that you have as you do that.

You can use these words to initiate that experience:

> "I am a wonderful human being. Life on earth is for *joy*, and *happiness*, and *love*. In this moment, I turn my human power of thinking and feeling toward creating an inner experience of *goodness*. I will now *create* the truth within myself by creating feelings of joy, happiness, and love."

As you continue to create feelings of goodness and truth, you can use any focal point that helps you. You might create a memory of wonderful feelings that you have had in the past. You can create a visual image of something that is beautiful and inspiring to you. You might choose to imagine your soul as a perfect divine being who is pouring love into you. Use anything that helps you create an inner experience of goodness during this stage of the transformation process.

As you carry out this stage over time, you will gain practice in creating goodness. Then, eventually, as you train yourself, the time that you spend creating feelings of goodness will begin to balance out the time that you have spent using your inner power to create negative feelings. Perhaps a time will come when you will actually spend more time each day creating the inner experience of goodness that reflects the truth of life, than you do creating negative feelings that grow out of human challenges, confusion, and fear.

You need not expect to entirely *eliminate* your negative feelings. We all will find something in life that will stir up those kinds of feelings now and then. But, as you work with this process of transforming your negative feelings, you will stop accepting those feelings as truths about yourself and your life. Then you will be able to move toward mastering your negative feelings.

The reason that it is so important to master your negative feelings is that they obscure the true goodness of you. And, they squeeze the joy out of being you.

Each day, you have the power inside your totally

unique reality—your private subjective experience—to *create* the inner experience that you desire, and to cease creating the experience that you do not like. In every day of your life on earth, you have the power to create feelings of goodness.

Events in the outer world come and go. *You* are permanent. You are a human self that after your physical death will realign with the permanent reality of you as an eternal soul.

When you work with this process of transformation to live through your negative feelings, release them, and then create feelings of the truth, you will clearly demonstrate to yourself that *no negative feeling of any kind, no matter how terrible, can ever diminish or damage your being*. The more that you work with this process, the more confident you will become that you can heal any negative feelings that you create.

To keep encouraging yourself in this work, and to remind yourself of the truth, you can say the following words to yourself as often as you like:

> "I have had some challenges in this lifetime that have stirred up my negative feelings. But, I am now learning to transform those feelings. I am beginning to understand that all negative feelings are *temporary*. The human life that I am living is aligned with my soul, and my soul is *eternal*. Therefore, *I* am eternal. The work that I am doing in this complicated human world, even though I may not clearly see it yet, or know the full extent of it, is a *mastery of life* that is important to me, to my soul, and to all souls."

In the spiritual realm, your soul "automatically" has a full awareness of the ongoing eternal experience of goodness. But, you as a "child" of your soul, are being trained to *create* that awareness through your own experience in the physical world. By transforming your negative feelings when they occur, and by practicing creating feelings of the truth, your awareness of the goodness of life will expand.

Remind yourself often that the largest truth is that *you are an eternal being* who has lived many human lifetimes on this earth. In those lifetimes, your human selves have had many negative thoughts and feelings, and *none* of them have ever diminished or damaged your being. And, *they never shall.* You will continue undiminished on your pathway of mastery of human life on earth through creativity, joy, and love.

Thinking this way as you carry out the transformation process will open the way for the full awakening of your Extraordinary Awareness. And that will help you move along on your pathway of enlightenment.

Chapter 12

The Ninth Key: Opening Your Intuition

---- ❈ ----

As you continue to work with the expansion of your emotional life, and the transformation of your negative feelings, you will be freeing your intuition from any limitations that you might have created in your emotional patterns. That prepares you for the expansion of your intuitive ability so that you can open your Extraordinary Awareness and learn to perceive your soul and the spiritual realm. Thus, you will move toward more enlightenment by working with the ninth key to higher consciousness, which is: *Opening your intuition*.

In the broadest sense, you can think of intuition as *your ability to sense something that is not available to your ordinary physical senses*—your sight, your hearing, your touch, your taste, your smell. It is an innate sensing faculty that you have to *inwardly* perceive what is not apparent in the outside physical world.

Opening your intuition is important in your work to experience your soul and the spiritual realm because spiritual realities have *non*-physical forms that cannot be perceived by your five physical senses. You will perceive those non-physical spiritual forms through your intuition.

When you are focused on what you perceive with your five physical senses, you are using your ordinary awareness. When you begin to perceive through your intuition, you are shifting to your Extraordinary Awareness.

Not only can you think of your intuition as an inner ability that you have within your human self, but you could also think of it as *a set of unique inner experiences* that you can have under certain conditions. Usually, one of those conditions is the creation of a dedicated period of time during which you ignore your ordinary thoughts and feelings about life. This means that you turn your attention away from the distractions of the outside physical world, and you turn your attention *inward*.

When you learn to do that you will experience your intuition as a *feeling* of something that you cannot verify through the usual means of collecting tangible evidence. So, you might say: "I sense something that I do not have evidence for. I do not have proof of its existence. But, I have a strong intuitive sense of its existence."

Proving that something exists in a real way in your ordinary daily life is usually a matter of verifying its existence in the physical world, within time and space. Such proof is gained through your five physical senses. To "prove" the existence of something that is *not* physical, something that exists *beyond* time and space, such as your soul, requires using something other than your physical senses. It requires the use of your intuition.

Thus, learning what really exists in normal life grows out of an interaction between your human self and the outer world. Your perception of the existence of non-physical realities, such as your soul, will occur within *your inner experience*. Your inner experience is not limited by time and space, although you might think that it is. In your inner experience, through the use of your imagination and your intuition you can go anywhere.

Your ordinary human experience rests upon trusting what you see with your own eyes, and the knowledge that you gain about other people and the physical world through your physical senses. All of that experience affects the way that you create your thoughts, feelings, and beliefs about life. If you can verify something as "real" through that process, then it becomes your "reality." Clearly, it is wise for all of us to respect that process and to live harmoniously within the objective reality of the physical world.

Yet, we are learning that our subjective human perceptions can be stimulated by real facts in the physical world, and then at times can go *beyond* those facts. For example, imagine that you are a person who cannot see well without your glasses. As you walk in a park, without your glasses, someone on the path in front of you drops a large orange and it rolls past you very fast. In your blurred vision, what you see is a tiny, fuzzy, orange kitten running past you. You love cats, and for a moment you have a very joyful feeling from seeing the kitten run by you. For that moment, that is your "truth." You are enjoying an orange kitten *in your inner experience.*

Even though your enjoyable personal experience does not change the physical orange into a physical kitten, you have still had a meaningful inner experience that was stimulated by the outer event. The outer event was the reality in the physical world. Your inner "reality" was an experience that was stimulated by your physical seeing of the orange, transformed by your imagination linked with your feelings about cats, all occurring within your subjective self.

The challenge that you face when you begin to open your intuition to perceive that which is non-physical, such as your soul, is the intelligent *integration* of the facts of the outer world with intuitive experiences of the inner life. If you would say: "I wish to *prove* that I just saw an orange kitten," you could speak to the person in front of you who dropped the orange. That person who was looking at the physical facts, and not seeing through your blurred vision, would inform you that what you saw was actually an orange rolling along the path.

Even though you now know the truth of that

physical event, it does not change the "truth" of the enjoyable inner experience that you just had of seeing a kitten. That inner experience does not suddenly become *not* real because it was stimulated by an orange. Clearly, the kitten that you saw was not physically real, but *your inner experience of the kitten was very real.*

The outer world can present you with objective facts, and it beneficial for all of us to live by and master those facts of daily life. However, the outer world of facts can also stimulate subjective experiences within us that can go beyond the facts. Those inner experiences are no less "real" to us because they do not match the facts that stimulated them. As long as we do not believe that our inner experiences are objective facts that everyone else must see, we can continue to use the facts of the outer world to stimulate inner experiences that go beyond the physical reality.

As you open your intuition, the important thing is to make certain that your inner experiences do not cause you to lose sight of the objective facts of the physical world. For the most successful and fulfilling life, we need to intelligently *integrate* our inner life of subjective experience with our outer life in the world of physical facts.

As you expand your intuition and you begin to have inner experiences that you believe to be meaningful intuitive perceptions, it will usually be difficult to prove the "truth" of those experiences, unless they relate to some tangible facts in the physical world that you can verify through a bit of research. Therefore, you will need to be aware that what you believe that you are perceiving through your intuition is an affair of your inner world, and those perceptions need to be examined with intelligence, in terms of your relationship with the outer world.

When you are not able to "prove" your inner perceptions in the usual way that you prove the existence of something in the physical world, you might find yourself confused. To work with any such confusion that might arise, you can remind yourself: "I live in a physical world. Therefore, no matter how I might subjectively perceive inner experiences, I am wise to first consult what I know about reality in the physical world to make certain that my inner experiences are not drifting off into personal fantasy." Then, after you do that and you are satisfied that you are not being misled by your inner experiences that are arising from the opening of your intuition, you can begin to allow those experiences to take you beyond the facts of the physical world.

Your body perceives the physical reality through its five senses and establishes the factual truth by which you live. Your mind and emotions respond to the factual, objective reality of the physical world as it is presented to you through your senses, and those responses create your inner subjective experience in relation to the facts of the physical world. Your *imagination* can *extend* your subjective experience beyond the ordinary limits associated with the physical world. However, your imagination is usually limited to what you consciously know, based upon your knowledge and experience of the physical world.

If you would say: "Let me imagine a four-headed giraffe," to do that accurately you must have had an experience of a *one*-headed giraffe in order to imagine a four-headed one. On the other hand, if you would say: "Let me imagine an *arkasenotolous*," (a made-up word), and you have never encountered such a creature, you could try to use your imagination to create an experience of the creature, but the experience would be quite jumbled, or confused, or, you might not be able to imagine it at all.

So, this brings us to intuition. The "mechanism" that you have within your human self for sensing that which goes beyond the normal is your intuition. You can intuitively sense that which you cannot imagine because your intuition has a far broader range than your imagination. Therefore, *your intuition can come closer to the non-physical realities of life than your imagination can.*

As you begin to open your intuition, and you are satisfied that you are well balanced in your daily life in the physical world, you need not limit yourself to what you have learned about reality in the physical world. Through your intuition you can begin to sense non-physical realities, such as your soul, that are not constrained by the same limits that exist in the physical world.

For example, in the physical world, you are not likely to see, with your physical eyes, a divine being of light walking toward you and then embracing you.

That would defy the "laws" of reality in the physical world. However, drawing upon your intuition that is not constrained by such laws, you could actually sense your own soul coming toward you and embracing you with its love in a very real way. You could not "prove" that your soul was real, but with the full opening of your intuition you could *verify*, through your own inner experience, that your soul was actually embracing you and loving you.

In your work to open to an experience of your soul, if you rely upon your ordinary experience of the physical world to determine what is *real*, then if your soul does not present itself in a way that you can see, touch, hear, taste, or smell, you must conclude that your soul is not real. On the other hand, if you call upon your awakened intuition, you can become aware of the *real* presence of your soul as a powerful force of love that is touching your feelings and your inner sensing.

Using your intuition to become more enlightened, you can eventually learn to sense the real presence of divine goodness everywhere. If you see a beautiful child who touches your heart, and you begin to feel a precious goodness in that child, you could say: "This is my soul touching my intuition to remind me that the goodness of the divine lives in every human." You could consider that to be a "message" from your soul that you perceived through your intuition.

❖

You can imagine the non-physical reality of your soul, but that imagining would be dominated by your perceptions that are rooted in physical reality. Just as you could imagine a four-headed giraffe if you have seen a one-headed giraffe, you could try to imagine your soul as a *being*, but your imagining would be based upon your perceptions of the beings that you are used to seeing in the physical world, which are human beings. The being of your soul would be equivalent to an *arkasenotolous*, and you have never seen one of those because they do not have a physical form that appears in your world.

If you try to go beyond your imagining of your soul, you will usually need to equate your soul with something that you are familiar with that is not physical. So, you might say: "Let me imagine my soul as an invisible *energy*." However, human ideas about invisible energies are rooted in realities in the physical world, and those realities are usually based on scientific concepts of invisible energies such as microwaves, ultraviolet energies, and so forth.

With your physical perceptions, your thoughts, your feelings, and your imaginings, you can only come to an approximation of your soul and the spiritual realities. It is only through intuition that you can come closer to the truth of those realities.

However, since intuition, in most people, is kept in the background of their awareness, they will not usually have deep intuitive experiences of the spiritual realities. This means that you must learn to work with your thoughts, feelings, and imagination to stimulate the expansion of the intuitive ability that you already have within your human self. By using your thoughts, feelings, and imaginings in periods of receptive, loving attunement, you can learn to draw your intuitive ability from the background of your human experience into the foreground. Then you can learn to intuitively perceive your soul in a way that goes beyond the physical, mental, emotional, or imaginative.

To expand your intuition you can draw upon the power of imagination as a *starting* point. Through the use of your imagination, you can project yourself beyond the limitations of the physical world. In time, as you open your Extraordinary Awareness and move closer to an experience of the spiritual realm, in addition to projecting your imagination, you can learn to actually project your *being*.

For example, if you wish to visit the planet Mars, you can sit quietly with your eyes closed and you can imagine such a visit. Even though you might inwardly create an accurate visual image of Mars, based on photographs of the planet that you have seen, you would realize: "This is simply imagination." You would know that you are not really visiting Mars. You would understand that you are not actually leaving the physical reality that you are used to. You would still be bound to your ordinary human experience that is limited to the physical locations that you can visit by walking to them, or by going to them in a vehicle.

Thus, in the physical sense, in terms of what you can do with your body in the physical world, you could say that you are "trapped" in the ordinary. However, you are not limited in that way in your inner life. In your inner life, you are not limited by anything. In your inner life, you can freely choose to grow wings and fly to Mars. And, that experience does not need to be less "real" because it begins as an imagination.

The more that you learn to imagine freely during periods of silent attunement, the more you can create a certain kind of inner release from the ordinary world. If you do that consistently for a period of time, you will learn to use your intuition to create experiences that are *initiated* by your imagination, but then go beyond that in a way that is not limited by physical reality.

By linking your imagination with a certain inner disengagement from your ordinary awareness, you can learn to create a special feeling and intuitive sensing that is actually an *energy adjustment* that is made inside your human self. That energy adjustment can gradually move your consciousness from perceiving through your ordinary awareness that is linked with your imagination that is based on your physical senses, to perceiving through your intuitive ability that is linked with your Extraordinary Awareness.

Such an intuitive opening will enable you to transcend the limitations of perception that are imposed upon your human self by your physical body. That will enable you to expand your personal "window of awareness" from which you look out upon the world.

Your window of awareness is usually dominated by your physical perceptions, and your usual thoughts and feelings about the physical world. That is what creates your ordinary awareness. Through inner experiences initiated by imagination, but then *expanded into a new energy configuration by your intuition*, you can actually begin to move and expand your window of awareness until you are perceiving through your Extraordinary

Awareness. Eventually, you can actually learn to project your awareness beyond the physical world in a very real way.

In time, as you become adept at this expansion process, your intuitive perceptions could actually expand into the physical space around you, just as mine did in the experiences that I described for you in an earlier chapter. Your perceptions could then go far beyond your physical location in that moment. Then, your inner perceptions—of course, not your body—could actually cross physical distance and arrive at the physical planet Mars. That would be accomplished through intuitive perception, not through using your five physical senses to perceive.

If you were to accomplish such an intuitive perception, it would not be imagination. It would be an inner perception, disengaged from the physical eyes through which you normally look. *You would be using your intuition to project your awareness beyond the human in order to peer through the eyes of your soul.* Your soul can perceive in any direction, in any realm, in any dimension, without the limitations of time and space.

Such an experience would begin by the creation of a feeling of freedom to disengage from your normal human perception of the world. It would come from an inner movement in which you would take your window of awareness of life out of its ordinary "position" that is rooted in physical reality, and you would lift it "above" the limitations of the physical world. Using your intuitive sensing, you would penetrate the veil of human opaqueness that normally enshrouds your perceptions. You would move through that veil and you would perceive the larger reality of life beyond the limits of human perception.

Using your intuition in a fuller way requires you to take special periods of time in which you turn your attention away from your usual preoccupation with your strong subjective experiences that are the ordinary reality that fills your awareness day after day in the human world. A preoccupation with your usual thoughts, feelings, desires, interests, and physical perceptions of life is linked with the self-directed use of your will that is necessary for you to accomplish what you desire in the physical world.

That focus is part of your normal human striving for what you want to create in your life in the outer world. While that is important to continue in order for you to have success in your daily life, it is "counter-intuitive." It draws your attention away from the more subtle, more refined aspects of reality that cannot be *attained*, but must be *sensed* with your intuition. Therefore, it is important to have special periods of time when you step back from the usual affairs of your daily life to put aside the dominating influence of your ordinary awareness. During those periods you can practice opening your intuition as a way of shifting to your Extraordinary Awareness.

When you begin to perceive your soul and the spiritual realities through your intuition, to actually *know* and be *aware* that you are sensing your soul, there needs to be something tangible for you to be aware of. Otherwise, your experience would be "blank." You need to have some kind of feeling or inner perception in order to consciously know that you are sensing your soul. Since a pure intuitive experience has no tangible "content," then the truth of spiritual realities that you perceive through your intuition needs to be "translated" into thoughts, or feelings, or an inner sensing of some kind.

After you learn to expand your intuition and you become familiar with releasing your perceptions from the strong influence of your usual physical sensations, thoughts, and feelings, you might at first simply experience a vague sense of peace. Then, an inner wisdom that you have beneath your conscious awareness, along with invisible impulses from your soul, can creatively translate your imperceptible intuitive experience into a tangible experience of some kind.

For example, you might actually have an inner vision of your soul. But that vision would be different from one that you simply created in your imagination. In your imagination you would be limited by what you already know about the realities in the physical world. You can only imagine a giraffe. You cannot imagine an *arkasenotolous*.

When you have a *true* intuitive sensing of your soul that is then translated by your inner wisdom, along with assistance from your soul, the vision of your soul that you would see in your mind's eye would be something that you could not imagine. It would be much closer to the truth of your soul than a simple imagination that is created without intuitive perception.

There *are* truths about your soul and the spiritual

realities of life. They have their own existence, their own nature, their own extraordinary qualities. Through intuitive perception you can come close to those truths.

The process for expanding your intuition involves *creating a feeling sense of leaving behind your normal thoughts and feelings about what you do in the world.* In this step, you can create a period of silence each day during which you begin to give up the self-preoccupied aspect of you. You can imagine that you are turning your full attention away from your ordinary inner experiences that are dominated by your pursuits in the physical world, and you will gently turn your attention to a feeling of being a more sensitive person than you usually feel that you are.

During this silent period your goal is to release the strong, dominating influence of the powerful thoughts and feelings that you use in your daily life to accomplish what is important to you. You will allow all of that to slip away from your awareness. You will turn your focus inward to a kind of inner sensing that is not related to your experience in the physical world. You will try to sense a kind of soft inner movement of something that is not physical, but that is infused with feelings that are deep and true. What you will be opening to in the creation of such new sensations is an inner aspect of your human self that I call "the intuitive sensing capacity."

I believe that we all have such an intuitive sensing capacity. It is an aspect of an inner magnificence and wisdom that you could think of as your true self, or your "higher" self. That is the core of your human self that is projected into you, and sustained by, your soul. When you learn to make the sensitive, receptive adjustment of your experience that I am trying to describe, there will come forth that powerful intuitive capacity that lives within you. It is always within you, but it is rarely in your conscious awareness.

It is difficult to accurately describe in words the inner sensation of releasing ordinary thoughts and feelings to gradually become aware of this intuitive sensing capacity. It is a subtle kind of feeling, or vague sensing. If you use my words as a starting point, and then practice in your own way in a daily period of silence, eventually you will begin to feel this sensation and you will realize that you are beginning to use your intuitive sensing capacity to create that experience.

As you learn to stimulate your intuitive sensing capacity in this inner practice of deep receptivity, your normal thoughts, feelings, and desires that are related to your usual self-preoccupation in the physical world will slip into the background. You can have experiences that link some new thoughts and feelings to the subtle reality of your inner wisdom within your true self. That can lead to an expanded awareness of yourself and your life. You will be stimulating your intuitive sensing capacity in a way that will enable you to begin to gain beneficial information about yourself and your life that goes beyond your ordinary thoughts and feelings. You could call that "inspired wisdom" from your true self.

For example, imagine that you are struggling with confusion about what to do with your life. You have many different thoughts and ideas about what you might do, but you cannot decide what would be best. You question yourself, and ponder the possibilities for months, but you cannot decide what is best for you.

After practicing releasing your normal thoughts and feelings in a silent attunement over a period of time, you could begin to sense that intuitive aspect of yourself in such a clear way that you could bring your troubling question into that inner intuitive experience. In that deepened state you could ask yourself: "What is best to do with my life?" You could then be penetrated with a new, inspired understanding of your dilemma that comes from your intuitive capacities that are an aspect of your true self. As a result, you could have brilliant new thoughts and feelings about what to do with your life.

Learning to open your intuition is a matter of making these kinds of inner adjustments so that you can come to a moment in which your awareness is not dominated by your old habits of thinking and feeling that are rooted in the "facts" of the physical world. As you make those adjustments, it becomes possible for your intuitive abilities to be impregnated by the wisdom of your true self, and that wisdom can rise up into your conscious awareness.

Another way to practice opening your intuition is to sit in a period of silence each day and train yourself to turn your attention entirely away from yourself. You can do that by simply thinking about other people. It is good to focus upon specific people that you know, instead of humanity in general. For example, you might begin to think about a dear friend and what they are doing in their life. You can remember everything that you know about that person and focus your entire thinking and feeling on that person for a few minutes.

As you do that, create a feeling of warmth and love for the other person. That will begin to lift you out of the "self-preoccupation mode" that we all live in most of the time. That will enable you to loosen your personal "knot of ordinary consciousness" that is usually tied so tightly around your thoughts and feelings that your intuitive sensing cannot break through. Focusing on another person in a loving way while you give up your normal thoughts and feelings in a deeply receptive state of consciousness will free your intuitive sensing from the constraints that bind it in daily life.

When you pay attention to other people, and you use your emotions to feel them deeply, understand them, care for them, and love them, it triggers a certain "mechanism" in your personality self energy structure that is not physical. It sets into motion a *non*-physical energy that triggers an actual physiological response in your brain. That stimulates certain capacities of your brain to shift to your Extraordinary Awareness, opening the way for your awareness to leap the gap between perceptions rooted in your physical experience in ordinary reality, to intuitive perceptions of the spiritual realm.

Thus, on your path of enlightenment, there is usually a certain beneficial and satisfying acceleration that occurs in your experience when you are sensitive to other people, and when your relationships with them are deep and meaningful. On the other hand, there is usually a certain "retardation" of the enlightenment experience when your self-preoccupation is too strong.

As you practice turning your attention away from yourself to focus on another person, your intense subjective engagement with your ordinary thoughts and feelings will temporarily be put aside, leaving room for your feelings to begin to register intuitive impulses from your true self that have been blocked by your constant focus on your own thoughts and feelings. In a way, you will begin to "ride upon" the feelings toward others that you are creating. You will begin to come out of your intense subjectivity, and, in an intuitive sense, you can go out to the person that you are focusing on.

You can use these words to facilitate this process:

> **"Casting myself out toward another person lifts me out of my limited, self-focused thoughts and feelings. It clears the way for my emotional capacities to become free to receive beneficial impulses that are not dominated by my ordinary self-preoccupied habits. It opens the way for powerful intuitive sensings to emerge from my true self. It also enables me to be receptive to intuitive promptings from my soul."**

Your intuition is the "conduit" through which the divine forces of your soul flow into your personality self structure. Your intuition makes those divine energies available to your thoughts and emotions so that they can become inspired beyond your own ordinary experience.

Thus, as you use the twelve keys to become more enlightened, you can draw upon your intuition to tap in to a vast storehouse of knowledge that your soul has. Ordinarily, that soul knowledge is held beneath your conscious awareness. By opening your intuition, you can begin to sense that knowledge and become consciously aware of it. Then you can use it to gain wisdom about your daily pursuits, to answer your important questions about life, and to receive inspired guidance directly from your soul.

Chapter 13

The Tenth Key: Opening to Your Soul

---※---

Drawing upon all that you have learned in the previous chapters you are ready to begin the actual process of becoming aware of your soul and the spiritual realm through a daily practice of opening your Extraordinary Awareness. You will now work with the tenth key to higher consciousness, which is: *Opening to your soul*. This will be the joyful process that will move you along on your path of enlightenment.

To be most effective in your opening to your soul, you will need a simple method for consistently focusing your inner experience on your soul during periods of silence each day. The method that I will show you has been developed through my years of study of human consciousness and my personal experience in my own spiritual work. I have also incorporated what I have learned from years of teaching people how to expand their awareness. This method has been effective for myself and for many people, enabling us to have deep and meaningful spiritual experiences.

As I mentioned earlier, I call this method for opening to your soul an *attunement* because it involves a process of shifting your attention from the "energy frequency" of normal life and tuning in to the energy frequency of your soul. This attunement process specifically directs your inner experience toward the realm of your soul. It will enable you to bring your feelings and your intuitive sensing capacity into play to create a shift from your ordinary awareness to your Extraordinary Awareness.

I will describe the attunement method for you in detail. The purpose here is to clarify for you what an attunement is, and to explain each step of the process.

This method of attunement can be a basic starting point for learning to shift to your Extraordinary Awareness. After you practice with this method for a while and you begin to get familiar with making that shift, then you will be able to sense ways in which you can adjust and expand upon the basic steps of the process to create your own personal attunement experience that is perfect for you.

Each day, take twenty or thirty minutes to practice this attunement. If you feel that you cannot spare that much time, then begin with at least ten minutes a day. Even if you only do your attunement for a few minutes every day, that is better than not doing it at all.

The basic attunement process consists of seven

steps. These seven steps can eventually lead you to a deep and inspiring experience of your soul and the spiritual realm.

Step One. The first step in your attunement process will be: Creating a *sanctuary* where you can go each day to open to your soul. Find a place that is quiet and soothing. If there is a telephone, turn it off. Make sure that you will have privacy and will not be interrupted.

Create a feeling of sacredness about your sanctuary place. You might light a candle, or bring in some beautiful flowers. You might decorate a special chair, or maybe put up pictures that have a spiritual significance to you. Do whatever will help you feel that your sanctuary is a special, sacred place.

When you create a special sanctuary for your attunement process, you change the energy from the ordinary to the spiritual. You establish strong stimuli in your physical environment that prompt you to prepare for an experience of your soul.

When it is time to do your attunement, go to your sanctuary and sit comfortably in a position that you can hold for a while. Close your eyes and settle in to the present moment. Use what you practiced in your inner work of focusing on the present moment.

Before you start your attunement process, decide what you want to achieve with it and set your intention for that. There are two general areas of inner accomplishment that you can choose from. One is to achieve as deep an experience of your soul as you can. The second is to connect with your soul to receive specific information, guidance, or answers to questions about your life.

If you decide to focus your attunement on receiving specific knowledge and wisdom from your soul, then think about all of the various aspects of your life that you are interested in and pick an area that seems most important to you. You might want guidance in a certain relationship. You might desire more creativity in your work. You might ask for a greater understanding of your purpose in life.

After you have chosen the general area, then frame a specific request in your mind that you will make to your soul during your attunement. For example, your request might be: "I now ask for the wisdom to know what to do to deepen my love relationship." Or, you might say to your soul: "Please show me how to discover my true purpose in life and how to fulfill it." Hold your request for your soul in your mind as you go to step two.

Step Two. The second step of your attunement process will be *to release your physical body*. In this step, begin by noticing any tension in your body. Tension, or nervous movements send signals to your brain that stir up brain activity, making it difficult to release your awareness from your first channel of ordinary awareness.

Take a few deep breaths. As you exhale, tell yourself that you are breathing out all tension. Encourage yourself to release more tension each time that you exhale.

Tell yourself that your body is relaxing from head to foot, and with each breath you are becoming more and more relaxed. The more you practice this, the deeper you will go into relaxation.

Then, to continue the release of your physical body, imagine that you are slowly floating out of your body. Create a soft, gentle feeling of floating upward away from your body.

As you imagine that, make a strong statement to yourself that affirms your intention to free yourself from physical reality. For example, you could say to yourself:

> "I now completely release my physical body. I am free from the heaviness of my body. I now float in a safe and gentle softness above my body."

Step Three. The third step in your attunement process will be to *release your thoughts*. The distractions of your day to day life, such as your work, relationships, and money, can keep your thoughts focused entirely on the physical world. When you make your attunement to your soul, you will need to release your ordinary thoughts in order to shift to your Extraordinary Awareness.

Many people believe that they need to completely eliminate their thoughts to have a deep spiritual experience. That is not necessary. In fact, it may not be possible for us to stop thinking entirely.

However, you can learn to release your thoughts and not pay attention to them. You can choose to turn your *attention* away from your thoughts and allow them to slip into the background of your awareness. You might vaguely notice them, but your attention will be focused beyond them.

Begin the process of releasing your thoughts by first calmly *observing* them for a minute or two. Just accept whatever thoughts you have without doing anything about them.

Next, begin to imagine that your thoughts are becoming less strong. They can continue, but imagine that they are becoming weaker and weaker.

At the same time, just as you imagined floating away from your physical body, begin to imagine that you are floating away from your thoughts. You can imagine your thoughts as a ball of dense energy. Feel yourself floating above that ball of energy as your thoughts get weaker, like a voice fading in the distance.

As you practice this, you will discover that your attention is separate from your thoughts. You can learn to direct your attention beyond any thoughts that you are having, and the thoughts can continue on without you paying attention to them.

It might take a while to get the feeling of releasing your thoughts, but in time you will become adept at allowing any thoughts to run their course while you shift your attention away from them.

Step Four. The fourth step of your attunement process will be to *release the physical world*. Here, you will use the power of your imagination to launch your awareness beyond its ordinary limits.

Begin by imagining your awareness becoming lighter and freer. Feel that you are beginning to float toward the ceiling of the room that you are in.

Then, imagine yourself floating through the

ceiling. Tell yourself that there are no limits to your movement. Gently and slowly imagine yourself floating upward through the roof of the building.

Continue on and imagine yourself floating entirely free of the building. Feel yourself easily, effortlessly floating up into the air, above your building, feeling safe and secure in your new freedom.

Then, imagine yourself floating even higher into the sky. As you go higher, feel a great sense of freedom and joy. All heaviness will fall away, and you will feel a wonderful lightness within you. At this point, tell yourself that you are free to soar into the beauty and magnificence of an amazing world beyond the physical reality.

Then, imagine that you are moving toward a most radiant and beautiful light. Imagine yourself coming closer and closer to this wondrous realm of light. Allow yourself to sense that the light is filled with warmth and love. Feel it emanating a comforting sense of love.

Next, imagine yourself floating *into* the light, as though you are entering a huge, radiant light cloud of bliss and love. As you enter this extraordinary realm of light, feel that you leave everything in the physical world behind.

Tell yourself that you are entering a spiritual realm of pure love. This is the realm of your soul.

Step Five. The fifth step of your attunement process will be to *connect with your soul*. You will accomplish this through the continued use of the power of your imagination, linked with your feelings and intuitive sensing.

As you imagine yourself floating in the majestic realm of light and love in the previous step, begin to feel that the love surrounding you is growing stronger. Feel that the love is beginning to flow *into* you. Where before it was enveloping you, now feel it completely filling you.

After you have saturated yourself with these feelings of love, begin to feel that the love is coming from a *presence* near you. Using the power of your imagination, feel that out of the loving light around you, this presence is coming forth toward you.

Gradually, begin to realize that this presence is your own soul. It is your soul that is loving you in such a profound way. Imagine your soul coming to you and embracing you with its limitless love. Feel the wonderful presence of your soul surrounding you and filling you with perfect love.

Tell yourself to open your heart fully so that you can allow the love to fill you. Take in the love calmly, without trying, or striving. Simply allow the love from your soul to fill you. Receive it with great appreciation and gratitude.

Step Six. In the sixth step of your attunement process *you will receive what you desire from the vast resources of your soul.* You will take in wonderful gifts of love and inspiration from your soul.

Begin by feeling that your soul is asking you what you want in your life. Imagine your soul speaking to you within your inner being in ways that you can *feel*.

Then, feel that your soul is offering you the

unlimited knowledge, talents, and abilities that it has within it. As your soul extends this invitation to you, say to yourself:

> **"I now release myself into the loving guidance of my soul. I ask my soul to help me expand my awareness so that I can have a profound and inspiring experience of the majesty of my soul, and the beautiful, loving radiance of the spiritual realm."**

If you want to receive specific knowledge or information from your soul, bring forth the clear request that you framed in the first step of your attunement, and say that statement to your soul. Whatever you decide you want from your soul, inwardly speak your statement of desire to your soul.

After you have done that, open yourself to receive what you have requested from your soul. Feel that within you there is a profound receptivity. Become poised and ready to take in the gift that you have requested from your soul.

That gift may come immediately, not as words, but as an inner knowing or feeling that illuminates the area that you asked about. You might feel a strong creative desire, or an impulse to take a certain action in that area. In that case, simply absorb what you receive, allowing it to sink into your consciousness.

It is possible that the gift from your soul will be planted as a seed that will grow and blossom at a later time. Later on, you could receive a profound inspiration and illumination as you are going about your daily affairs. Or, you might have a dream that will bring you a full revelation of the gift that you received from your soul during your attunement.

Whatever you experience in this step of your attunement, be entirely passive and *receive* it. Let it flow into you without any effort on your part. Allow it to penetrate you fully, along with the love from your soul. Know that you have received a wonderful gift that will continue to grow as you work day by day to expand your awareness even further.

Step Seven. The seventh step in your attunement process will be *to bring the gift from your soul back to your ordinary world*. In this step, you will return to your normal awareness of yourself in the physical world.

It is very important to do this step slowly. Always take as much time as you need to return to your ordinary state of awareness without rushing yourself. If you rush this step, you can become confused or disoriented when you come out of your attunement.

Begin this step by thoroughly absorbing whatever you experienced in the period of receiving from your soul. Make a mental note of anything that you learned or absorbed. Let any inspired thoughts, ideas, or feelings that you received from your soul sink in so that you can retain them and bring them back with you. Tell yourself that you will remember all that you need to remember about what you received from your soul.

Then, just as you imagined yourself floating into the radiant light and love of the spiritual realm, now imagine yourself slowly withdrawing from that realm. Feel that you are gently drifting out of the light. Allow the light to begin to gradually recede into the distance.

As this occurs, know that the love of the spiritual realm remains with you. *Feel* that love within you.

Then, imagine yourself drifting easily and comfortably toward the earth and back into the physical world. Feel yourself coming closer and closer to earth until you return back through your roof and ceiling to hover over your physical body.

With a sense of ease and effortlessness, imagine yourself slipping back into your physical body. Feel comfortable and relaxed. Feel yourself becoming perfectly integrated with your physical body. Feel solid and secure within your body.

Finally, begin to completely release yourself from your expanded awareness. Allow that awareness to slowly drift away. Feel yourself re-engaging your ordinary thoughts and feelings, and calmly turn your attention to your physical surroundings. Notice how the air feels. Notice any sounds that you might be hearing.

Then, turn your attention to your body. Become very aware of how your body feels in that moment. Slowly begin to move your fingers, then your toes. Tell yourself that you are perfectly balanced and secure within your body, that you are feeling very refreshed and rejuvenated, and that you are fully alert to your surroundings.

Sit quietly for a minute and experience a sense of inspiration and rejuvenation. Then, when you feel ready, slowly open your eyes.

Look around until you regain your sense of being fully centered in your body. When you feel ready, stand up and stretch your body. Then, joyfully return to your physical life with enthusiasm and renewed inspiration.

One distraction that might come up when you are doing your attunement is the tendency to constantly check on yourself during your attunement to try to see how you are doing, to see if you are having a deep experience yet. When you do that, you will usually discover that you are not feeling anything special. You will just feel ordinary. That is because the process of using your mind to check up on yourself engages your ordinary awareness and limits your experience of the moment. That blocks your shift to your Extraordinary Awareness. If you continually observe your experience to see how it is going, you can come to feel that your attunements are never successful, and you can get very frustrated.

If you catch yourself checking to see how you are doing, do not fight it. Just calmly witness it with a loving sense of patience. Then, turn your attention away from that and remind yourself that you are not working at your attunement to get results. You are just having a relaxing, enjoyable experience in the present moment. You can then gently release the desire to evaluate or assess the experience of that moment.

We are all trained to make progress in the physical world by getting *results*. Once we get one result, we are off to achieve the next one. This constant striving for results points us toward the future. We establish a *habit* of continually rushing toward the future, and that habit prevents us from enjoying the creative process in the moment that is involved in achieving our results. We forget how to savor our daily activities for the joy of being engaged in them. We are so busy *doing* that we do not practice *being*.

I have learned this lesson in my own life through my expression as an artist. I paint solely for the joy of the experience of painting. Yet, sometimes when I am working on a canvas, I get caught up in striving for the result of finishing that painting. When I do that, I begin to inwardly push myself, and soon I am rushing to get the canvas done. Then, when that painting is finished, I find myself immediately hurrying to start another one, and then I rush to finish that one. In that frantic striving for results, I lose touch with the moment to moment joy of the experience of painting.

To break that habit, I have to consciously slow myself down and focus on what I am doing in the present moment—the actual process of doing the painting. When I do that, I recapture the real joy of being an artist, which is the experience of painting, not the end result of a completed work.

When you do your attunement, remind yourself that you want to engage your experience of the present moment, not strive for any particular result. Instead of pushing toward a spiritual experience, focus on enjoying the process of opening yourself to the spiritual realm. Allow yourself to savor the moment by moment joy of relaxing and releasing yourself into the love of your soul.

You can even learn to let go of caring whether you

consciously have a deep spiritual experience or not. You can simply relax and trust that your attunement experience of that moment is part of a deep inner opening in you that is taking place over a period of time. And know that your opening is being lovingly guided by your own soul.

As you do your attunement each day, remember that you do not need to be *perfect* as a person in order to experience the perfection of your soul. Even if during your day you have felt frustrated, troubled, or challenged, you can still do your attunement to expand your awareness and connect with the beauty and the love of your soul.

You soul is always with you, loving you and guiding you, whether you are making your attunement, or simply going about your daily activities. Your soul's love for you is a constant in your life, whether you are aware of it or not. The only variable is your human awareness of that love.

By working with this attunement process you will be able to shift to your Extraordinary Awareness more and more. That will enable you to become consciously aware of the love of your soul more often. Then, you will know that you are never alone at any time in your life. You will know that your soul is always loving you. That will become your guiding light along your pathway of enlightenment.

Chapter 14

The Eleventh Key: Creating an Ongoing Spiritual Focus

---- ✻ ----

After you learn to create your attunement experience through daily practice, you will have an effective method for shifting to your Extraordinary Awareness to experience the spiritual realm, and then returning to your ordinary awareness. The next key to higher consciousness will determine whether or not your attunement practice will be fully beneficial for you. That key is: *Creating an ongoing spiritual focus.* Your work with this key will be rewarded by a powerful spiritual connection that you can maintain on a continuing basis.

The most important factor in creating an ongoing

spiritual focus is *persistence*. This means persistence in doing your attunement process every day, and, persistence in creating a spiritual focus throughout each day outside of your attunement period.

Because we all have such intense and complex lives in the physical world, we can be inundated by the many activities and concerns that constantly occupy us. Our daily affairs involving work, money, relationships, and other pressing matters in the outer world fill our awareness from morning till night. All of that dramatic activity overshadows the more subtle realities of our inner life, leaving little room for an awareness of our soul and the spiritual realm. The powerful downstream current of ordinary awareness in the river of life is so strong that it can carry us away if we do not persistently give some attention to the spiritual realities.

Since there are so many distractions in daily life, it is extremely important to practice your full attunement each day, and then to give at least a bit of attention to the spiritual realm throughout your day. It can take time to learn to break through the normal human preoccupation with the distraction of the physical world, to get past the powerful influence of ordinary awareness to shift to your Extraordinary Awareness. Therefore, persistence in doing your attunement each day, and in creating a periodic focus on inner spiritual feelings during the day, will be critical factors in making that shift.

When you consistently do your attunement every day, you will begin to make an inner pathway to higher levels of consciousness. That path will become wider and clearer the more persistently you travel it.

This process can be symbolized by the simple image of a beautiful, clear pond that is surrounded by tall grass. One day, a wandering deer makes its way through the grass, discovers the pond, and stops to take a drink.

Where the deer has walked, the grass has been pushed aside and there is the beginning of a path. However, if the deer goes away and never comes back that way again, the grass will spring back and everything will be the same as it was before.

This represents a brief, sporadic attempt to attune to your soul. A lack of persistence creates a faint pathway through your ordinary awareness. The grass of daily distractions will spring back and everything will be the same as it was. If you are not persistent in doing your attunement every day, you will remain primarily focused on your ordinary awareness, just as you have always been.

If the wandering deer returns to the pond every day, pretty soon there will be a clear path cut through the grass. When you do your attunement every day, you create a clear path through your ordinary awareness that leads to higher levels of consciousness. This clears the way for the opening of your Extraordinary Awareness and an experience of your soul and the spiritual realm.

By persistently doing your attunement every day, you will become adept at shifting your attention to higher levels of consciousness. That will make the attunement process so satisfying that it will be a joy to do. Your persistence will pay off by taking any feeling of work out of the attunement. It will eventually become a pleasurable, deeply satisfying activity to do each day.

The second area in which persistence is important is in taking a spiritual perspective each day, outside of your formal attunement period. Even in your daily activities, you can take some time out to do a brief attunement for a minute in which think about your soul and your eternal nature. You can feel the wonderment of human life, and you can imagine the profound soul connections that you have with the people in your life.

During that brief attunement moment you can create a feeling of opening that is similar to what you experience during your full attunement period. Although that brief feeling will not be so strong because you are in your ordinary awareness, nevertheless, you can still feel some inspiration as you "mingle" your ordinary awareness with a bit of your Extraordinary Awareness.

If you are persistent in doing this momentary attunement several times a day, you will begin to create beautiful experiences that will inspire you. You will gain balance, harmony, and a sense of purpose in your daily life, even during a busy day. You will learn to slow down and pay more attention to the people around you. That can help you become aware of deep, loving connections that you have with the people in your life. Eventually, you can learn how those connections fit into the purposes that your soul has for your interaction with those people.

Here is a simple but effective way to bring the expanded awareness that you gain from your full attunement period into the activities of your daily life. Each day, as soon you wake up in the morning, before you get out of bed, take a minute to turn your attention to your soul and to the spiritual realm by doing the following five steps.

First. Briefly re-create the inspired feelings that you have when you are doing your full attunement. Create a feeling of relaxation, softness, receptivity, and love.

Second. Say this affirmation to yourself: "In this moment, I release all distractions of the physical world. I now open myself to the beauty and love of my soul. During the coming day, I will return to this feeling whenever I can."

Third. Imagine your soul in that moment working inside you to help you feel the loving connection that you have with your soul. Imagine a wonderful spiritual reality in which many souls are inwardly working with you to help you learn and grow in your human life. Included in that reality are the souls of the people in your life. Their souls are aligned with your soul to help you deepen your relationships with the people that you will interact with in the coming day.

Fourth. Let yourself feel how important it is that you are living as a human being on earth right now. You are expressing talents and abilities that have been placed into your personality self by your soul. Remind yourself that each day of your life is meaningful in ways that are important to your soul.

Fifth. Feel how important the people in your life are. You are drawn to certain people by strong impulses from your soul and from their soul. Therefore, there are very important purposes in your relationships with those people. During this moment of brief attunement, imagine what those purposes might be, and feel those purposes as deeply as you can. Then, affirm that, as you go forth into your day, you will create a sense of purpose in the interactions that you have with people in that day.

Every morning, do these five steps briefly, one after the other. The total time that you take can be from one to five minutes, depending on how busy you are.

Always do these steps easily, in a relaxed way, without straining or pushing. Make this brief shift to your higher awareness a pleasant activity that you enjoy, not another burdensome task that you feel that you must do in order to improve yourself as a person. This process will set a spiritual focus for the day, and you will be able to carry a feeling of inspiration into your daily activities.

Not only can you do this momentary attunement in the morning before you begin your day, but you can also use it as much as you want throughout the day to bring a spiritual focus into your ordinary activities in the physical world. You can write yourself notes as a reminder to do this brief attunement, or you can set a watch alarm to remind you. Each time that you do this brief attunement during the day, simply repeat the same five-step process that you did in the morning.

The more persistent you are in using this abbreviated attunement several times a day, the more powerful the results will be. You will discover that you can bring a deep spiritual perspective into any area of your life, and that perspective will enrich your overall experience.

The results of making this brief attunement during the day can be particularly satisfying in your relationships with other people. The daily interactions with others that you might have previously considered to be mundane and ordinary will take on a deeper significance as you begin to sense important purposes that are played out in those relationships. Where before you might have felt a lack of depth in some of your relationships, with the perspective that you achieve from this brief attunement, you will begin to discover profound levels of meaningfulness and love in your connections with the people who are important to you.

When you combine persistence in this brief, periodic attunement throughout the day with persistence in your full attunement period, you will create an ever-deepening experience of your soul and the spiritual realm. Being persistent in these two ways over a period of time will create an ongoing spiritual focus that will lead to the expansion of consciousness that will enable you to have a more frequent experience of your soul. That will become a powerful inner force of magnificence that will be available to you on your pathway of enlightenment.

Chapter 15

The Twelfth Key: Exercising Patience

---❋---

Even after you have worked with the other eleven keys to higher consciousness, you will discover that it takes time to learn to shift to your Extraordinary Awareness to become aware of your soul and the spiritual realm. That is why the twelfth key is so important. That key is: *Exercising patience in the practice of your attunement.*

Patience is much more than an idea. It is a *feeling* inside you. It is a feeling that you do not need to hurry, or rush to get where you are going. It is also a feeling of trust that where you are in your inner work is where you need to be in that moment. It can be a strong feeling of goodness about being wherever you are in the present moment. Most importantly, it is a feeling that what you are looking for is *with you*, not somewhere else.

If you learn to be patient in your attunement process, then you will be able to more fully engage the present moment. If you become impatient and begin to rush yourself, you will become distracted and will not be able to focus on your experience of the present moment. And, it is in *the present moment* that you will experience your soul.

When you do your attunement, whether in your formal period, or in the brief attunements that you make during the day, you might become impatient because you feel that your inner experiences are not dramatic enough, or as spiritual as you desire them to be. At times, you might feel that your enlightenment process is not moving fast enough. If you do not live through such feelings and regain the feeling of patience, you can become critical of yourself and feel that you are not able to make a successful attunement. That would discourage you and cause you to create feelings of frustration. Those feelings would create a *contraction* in your awareness that would block the expansion of consciousness that you are seeking. If you did not patiently adjust those feelings, you might become so discouraged that you would give up doing your attunements.

If you are willing to be patient with any feelings of disappointment about your attunement process and remember that they are only temporary feelings that you are creating, then you will be able to release those feelings and regain your confidence in your intuitive sensing ability. You will be able to continue to do your attunement each day in a confident, trusting manner. That will keep you moving along steadily on your pathway of enlightenment.

Not only do you need to be patient with the progress of your overall attunement work, but you also need to exercise your patience in each individual attunement period. When you are doing your attunement, at times you might notice that you are feeling flat and uninspired. That might cause you to begin to try to make an attunement happen. That would create tension that would block your opening.

If you notice that occurring, release the desire to force your experience to be different. Let go of any desire to achieve results in the attunement. Become passive and receptive, and allow your soul to help you deepen your experience in an easy, natural way.

As you learn to be patient with the various confusions that you create in your attunement work, you will move forward in your inner experience in a way that is best suited to your personal patterns and needs. Your soul will help you awaken you Extraordinary Awareness in the amount of time that serves you best. All the while, you can keep enjoying the peace and calm of each day's attunement without demanding that your experience be a certain way. Think of every attunement experience, whether simple or cosmic, as important steps on your path of enlightenment.

If you notice that you are becoming impatient with your daily attunement practice, you might want to take a few days off and release any feelings of *working* at your attunement. Give yourself some time to let go of your feelings of impatience so that you can once again feel relaxed about doing your attunements. Regain the pleasurable feeling of savoring the peace and calm of your attunement period without demanding that you have a certain kind of experience.

After that, return to your daily attunement practice with a renewed sense of joy and confidence. Know that simply being patient with each day's attunement is all that you are asking of yourself. You do not need to demand that you achieve anything special. Trust that each day that you attune to your soul, important inner accomplishments are occurring, even if they do not manifest as particularly dramatic spiritual experiences during your attunement period.

Even after you begin to have meaningful and inspiring experiences in your attunements, you will still need to exercise your patience. For example, in a certain attunement you might have a deeply moving experience of your soul loving you. Then, the next day you have the same experience. You feel very inspired. Day after day, you experience the same level of intensity of love from your soul. Then, after a period of time, when that experience becomes very repetitive and familiar, you might begin to feel impatient that it is not deepening even more. You could begin to take the experience for granted.

Taking things for granted happens a lot in our daily lives. For example, if we buy a new car, the first day that we have the car we are really excited about it.

We pay a lot attention to that new car, and we deeply appreciate it. But, when we drive that car day after day for many months, then it is not so thrilling anymore. We begin to take it for granted and we hardly notice it. We then begin to look for something new to be excited about.

In the same way, you can take your attunement experience for granted. After you begin to feel a connection with your soul, and then you repeat that same experience in your attunement day after day, the experience can seem too ordinary to be satisfying. If that happens, you can become impatient and begin to hunger for something new, something more exciting. That can cause you to wander away from a very important opening that is occurring during your attunement in the experience that you are taking for granted.

If you work patiently with your daily attunement experience and enjoy it for what it is, whether or not it seems new and exciting to you, your experience will eventually deepen by itself. You will not need to impatiently push yourself to create something new because your attunement experience seems too familiar or ordinary. You will be able to appreciate the experience that you have become familiar with and are taking for granted, and you can begin once again to simply enjoy the attunement moment without trying to make something happen.

There are two ways to exercise your patience and work with any attunement experiences that begin to seem ordinary because you repeat them day after day. The first method is to create some *appreciation* and *gratitude* for your inner accomplishments. Pay more attention to whatever you might be experiencing in your attunement, and try to stir up an intense feeling of thankfulness for the inner opening that you have achieved. Say to yourself:

> "I have made a great deal of growth in my attunement process, but I have become so familiar with it that it now seems ordinary. In this moment, I release all feelings of ordinariness, and I celebrate the important openings that I have made."

The second way to work with attunement experiences that seem flat and too ordinary is to lovingly monitor an inherent human tendency toward *self-diminishment* that we all have, and to become aware of the influence of that tendency on your attunement experience. Such a tendency can often cause *you* to feel ordinary, and then you will tend to project those feelings of ordinariness onto your attunement experience. You will believe that you are discontent with your attunement, when actually you are feeling discontent with yourself and your life. It is not really your attunement experience that is flat and uninteresting. It is that within yourself, you are feeling that *you* are uninteresting, or ordinary, or insignificant, or inadequate.

When you are in that place, you might unconsciously start to push toward new experiences in your attunements as a way of distracting yourself from your feelings of self-diminishment. That will block your growth, and eventually it will lead to frustration and feelings of failure in your attunement.

When you feel flat and unfulfilled in your attunement because you are feeling diminished within yourself, you need to be patient with those feelings, and you need to find a way to stir up new feelings of interest and enthusiasm. You need *inspiration*. The inspiration can prod you to go beyond your limited feelings about yourself.

The first way to inspire yourself is to find some benefit and purpose in your feelings of flatness and ordinariness. Remind yourself that certain periods of pausing that seem to you to be uninteresting, are actually very important rhythms in your attunement cycles. You can say to yourself:

> **"This calm period in my attunement is beneficial. I do not want to cut this short by rushing ahead to create a new experience. Instead, I will be patient and I will focus on this present experience, and truly enter it, and learn from it."**

If you begin to push for new openings to escape your feelings of self-diminishment, you will not fully benefit from the experiences that you are having. So, instead of striving for new inner openings as a way of distracting yourself from feeling ordinary, patiently savor every moment of your attunements even when you are feeling ordinary, and look for purpose and meaning in those moments.

If you can only find purpose and meaning in one kind of attunement experience that pleases you, then you are limiting yourself. When you can find purpose and meaning in the entire range of your attunement experiences, from the ordinary to the deeply inspiring, then you are truly mastering the attunement process. You are well on your way to the incredible benefits that will come from patiently expanding your consciousness and becoming more enlightened.

Chapter 16

Your Path of Enlightenment

❋

In the day to day practice of your attunement, you will be creating a path of enlightenment for yourself. That grows out of a personal dedication to continue to expand your awareness to include a larger reality than would normally appear to you in the ordinary world.

If you carry out that expansion of your awareness, and at the same time you create personal growth and love in your everyday life, you will take a journey straight into the heart of magnificence. Walking a path of enlightenment will literally transform your experience of the physical world, illuminating it, deepening it, and bringing you the fulfillment that you desire in your life.

❖

There are four important aspects of a fulfilling pathway of enlightenment that you need to be aware of.

First: Your willingness to consistently open yourself to experience more than ordinarily appears on the surface of physical life. This involves a continuing quest for deeper purpose and meaning in everything that you do.

Second: Setting aside a "sacred" time each day to expand your awareness of your soul. You will do that in your daily attunement period.

Third: Your personal dedication to consistently remain open in your daily activities to the loving influence of the spiritual realities that sustain human life. You can accomplish that by doing the brief attunement practice throughout your day that you learned in chapter 14.

Fourth: Your ongoing commitment to continually strive to bring together the *human* and the *divine* in every moment of your life. This involves the merging of *personal growth* with *spiritual enlightenment*.

Creatively integrating the human and the divine in your day to day life is vital to your path of enlightenment. If you sit at home alone and practice perfect divine love, but you never go out into the human world to love anyone, your pathway will be distorted. For the greatest mastery, not only do you need to discover truth in your inner life, but you also need to *act* on that truth in the outer world of other people.

❖

By dedicating yourself to these four aspects of your path of enlightenment, you begin to *choose* the direction of your life in a most powerful way, instead of allowing your days to unfold haphazardly under the influence of your ordinary habits of thinking and feeling.

Each day, as you go out into the world, it is as if you are boarding a ship for a journey toward your future. If you do not take command of that ship and choose where you want it to go, it might take a direction that you do not want to take. If you do not consciously choose what your path in life will be, and decide how you will use your creative forces to walk that path, you might find yourself using your talents and abilities in ways that take you in a direction that will not fulfill you.

For example, imagine that you are an office worker whose job is unsatisfying, but, you hang on to it because it seems too difficult to find another career that would be more fulfilling. Because of that, you do not choose a path. You simply allow old habits to choose for you. Thus, out of habit, you are boarding a ship of personality self expression that is taking you toward a future that will not completely fulfill you. Your talents and abilities are being used in ways that are not fully completing your life's purposes. In such a situation, it will be more difficult to attain the experiences of fulfillment that your soul intended for your human life.

When you walk a path of enlightenment in which you merge the human and the divine by bringing together your personal growth and your spiritual experiences, you are quite consciously choosing where the ship of personality self expression will take you in this lifetime. You are choosing to move toward a full expression of yourself in ways that will complete the important purposes that your soul has given you.

❖

To gain more clarity about where your present choices are taking you, you can ask yourself: "What kind of life path am I creating with my present habits of thinking and feeling? Where are my habits leading me? Are they leading me toward joy and fulfillment, or toward limit and incompletion?" If you do not notice where your habits are taking you, then they can dominate you. When you pay attention to your habits, you gain the power to *change* the ones that are leading you where you do not want to go in your life.

To remind yourself how your create your life, say this to yourself every morning when you get out of bed:

> **"The quality of my choices, my thoughts, and my feelings in this day will determine the quality of my *future days*. I create my life's path by the important choices that I make today."**

When you make the daily choice to walk a path of enlightenment, you are essentially making a commitment to bring your human personality into a clearer, stronger experience of spiritual realities. You are intentionally setting out to expand your awareness to gain a higher consciousness that leads to an experience of the divine forces of your soul.

Here are three important reminders that can help you achieve that higher consciousness as you walk your path of enlightenment day by day.

First. It will be important to have a willingness to *care more,* which eventually will stimulate you to be willing to *love more.* Loving begins with caring. You can care more about your own personality self and about your life path. You can care more about the people around you. You can stir up feelings of compassion, generosity, and kindness, to the best of your ability. Those areas will eventually blossom into feelings of love in your heart.

Second. Imaginatively *create a holy temple to which you assign yourself and dedicate yourself.* You might imagine that you are a mystical priest or priestess under holy orders, but *your temple is of your own creation.* It is *your inner experience.* You enter your temple when you inwardly bring your full consciousness to bear upon your soul, and upon the spiritual forces of life, whether that occurs in your formal attunement period, or in dedicated moments throughout your day. You take that sense of sacredness with you wherever you go.

Third. Make a commitment to a *direction* that has important purposes in the *outer* world. If you give all of your attention to your inner life, your spiritual pathway will lack purpose and meaning. You need to *do* something in the outer world of other people to truly bring your pathway into full brilliance.

A beneficial direction that you can choose in your life in the outer world is to decide to bring the *love* that you gain in your inner work into the lives of other people to benefit them in some way. You can participate in activities of teaching, generosity, and helping others in ways that you believe are meaningful. You might decide to write about, or speak about knowledge that you believe can inspire people. You can choose for yourself what actions to take in the outer world in order to give to other people. The important thing is to do *something* so that you do not become too inwardly directed as you work with the twelve keys, and as you do your attunement practice each day.

From time to time, it is wise to assess how you are doing on your path of enlightenment. You can make this assessment by establishing a *reference point*, then determining how far you have come in relation to that point.

A powerful reference point for this process is *a feeling of perfect love*. Although you may not always achieve such a feeling, you can use it as your highest ideal, then you can assess yourself each day to see how close you have come to that ideal.

When you do occasionally create a feeling of perfect love, you can assume that your human experience in that moment is very close to *divine truth*, for the energies of the spiritual realm have a harmony and perfection that you can understand as perfect love. On the other hand, when you are creating experiences of negativity, you will know that you have moved away from truth.

This is not to suggest that it is wrong or bad to have negative feelings. We all have them from time to time. Yet, in your assessment process, you can understand that *consistent* negative feelings are a signal to you that there is inner work to be done in order to move toward your ideal reference point.

If the perfect energies of your soul could flow into your personality self *unobstructed* by limited human thoughts and feelings, they would cause you to feel a constant ecstasy and unbounded love. As those soul energies are obstructed by the inherent limits of your human personality self, the intensity of such feelings of goodness decreases, and therefore you feel less love. If your soul energies were *fully* obstructed by your personality distortions, then you would have no positive feelings at all. Within your inner experience there would be a coldness and emptiness.

As a general guideline for assessing how you are doing on your path of enlightenment, you can say to yourself: "If my inner experiences are leading me toward love, then I am moving toward truth in my life. If those experiences continually lead me to negativity and pain, then I am moving away from truth."

Gently monitor, on the one hand, how much harmony, joy, and love you are creating in your inner and outer life, and, on the other hand, how much turmoil, pain, and suffering you are creating. That can help you become aware of any patterns that are blocking your pathway. It can also help you discover any imbalance between your inner life and your outer life that could confuse you on your spiritual journey.

For example, if you assess yourself and find that as you do your attunement each day you are opening to more truth in your inner life, but, in the outer world you are creating ongoing negativity and turmoil with other people, then you would clearly see that you are out of balance. You would understand that even though you may be making some beneficial openings in your attunement, you are not bringing forth those energies of truth into your outer life. In that case, to truly walk your path of enlightenment, you would need to give some attention to harmonizing your life in the outer world with other people.

If you feel that most of the time in your outer life you are creating harmony, balance, and a sense of love, then you can expect your inner life to reflect these accomplishments. When you do your attunement, you can expect to be able to align more easily with truth. If your outer life is consistently negative, then you might find it difficult to make the inner opening in your attunement that leads to a clear experience of your soul and the spiritual realm.

Your ability to walk a path of enlightenment and consciously align with truth depends upon your *motives*, your *thoughts* and *feelings*, your *beliefs* about life, your *relationships* with other people, and your *activities* in the outer world. By honestly and lovingly assessing yourself each day to see how you are doing in those areas, you can become aware of any disruptive patterns that need to be addressed and transformed, and, you can build upon the beneficial patterns that you find that help you move toward truth in your life.

When you assess your day to day creations, it will be very important not to *condemn* any negativity that you might be creating in your life. You want to look for ways to *transform* your negative creations, not condemn them. You can remind yourself of this by saying to yourself: "I will be patient and flexible with my self-assessment. It does not serve me to condemn myself. It serves me to patiently decide which of my daily creations open the way to truth, and which ones block the way."

Another important aspect of creating your path of enlightenment is your willingness to take *a higher vision* of your day to day life. If you wake up in the morning and say: "I have to go to work, run some errands, and pay some bills," that is an ordinary experience. If you do those things, you are making normal human accomplishments in the ordinary way, without much sense of how they relate to larger purposes in your life. You are simply following the natural human impulse to focus on the physical world in order to succeed in that world.

Such an approach to life can be important, but, if that is all that you do, then you will stay on the surface of life. You will not break through to the deeper purposes for your life on earth.

When you walk a path of enlightenment, you add something to the normal, ordinary impulse within you that prompts you to constantly focus on the physical world in order to master it. What you add is *an awareness of the deep, important purposes that your soul has for you while you are carrying out your daily tasks in the physical world.*

You can discover those important soul purposes simply by taking some time to look for them. For example, imagine that you wake up in the morning and you begin to go over your list of the ordinary things that you will do in the physical world that day. After you do that, you can use the power of your imagination to focus on the coming day in the *non*-physical world. In the world of yourself as a *soul*.

Here is an example of how that can be done.

Begin by imagining that you are your soul in that moment. Imagine yourself as your perfect soul observing your human personality self as it gets out of bed. From that higher perspective, begin to assess what your personality self is choosing to focus on and make important in that day.

Let us say that you see your personality self fretting about money, and making plans to get more money. Now, *you-as-a-soul* understand that money only exists in the physical world. There is no such reality in the realm of the soul. So, as you assess your human personality self and its plans for that day, you feel the need to say to your personality self: "If you keep focusing on money, that can bring you some temporary pleasure and joy, but, *nothing will be achieved that will be taken beyond death.*"

You-as-a-soul want your human personality self to create primarily in areas that are taken through the door of death into the spiritual realm. You understand that one of those areas is *love*. So, you say to your personality self: "The experiences of love that you have while you are in human form will become permanent energies that will extend beyond your death into eternal realms."

You-as-a-soul try to teach your personality self that the creation of human experiences of love is a deeper engagement of life than the pursuit of wealth. You try to convince your personality self to pay more attention to love.

This does not mean that the pursuit of wealth is wrong, or bad. That can be associated with experiences that have purpose and meaning for you. But, if you *only* focus on wealth, you will not create the depth in your life that your soul desires for you. If you add love to your pursuit of wealth, then you can create that depth.

You-as-a-soul might also try to teach your personality self that an obsessive focus on *sensual pleasure* does not create the ongoing sense of purpose and meaning that you need in your life. For example, if you have an intense desire to eat a steak, in that moment a steak might seem like the most important thing in the world to you. But, if you eat the steak, then afterward a steak is not so interesting to you. You do not sit around feeling: "My purpose in life is to eat steaks."

By occasionally taking this larger perspective of your soul, you can learn to transcend the limits of sensual pleasure to focus on higher experiences that can bring deep purpose and meaning into your life. For instance, if you have sex with someone, after you are fully satiated, you are not likely to feel: "Having sex is the purpose of my life." However, if you focus on a higher experience of deep love for that person with whom you had sex, you might feel: "Loving this person in a deeper way is an important purpose in my life."

I am not suggesting that you criticize yourself for having certain goals that relate to sensual fulfillment. Such fulfillment can be very important in everyone's life. If you do not have enough sensual fulfillment you can begin to feel that there is no joy in your life. But, if your entire focus is on sensual pleasure, you are cheating yourself. You are missing the profound purposes for which you came into earth life in the first place.

If you want to discover those important soul purposes in your life and begin to fulfill them, you will need to bring more *depth* into your daily experience. Depth is the opposite of superficial sensual pleasure. The superficial areas of life are temporary. Depth has to do with meaningful *long-term* experiences. Those long-term experiences are related to such permanent expressions as, idealism, truth, honor, growth, honesty, and connectedness to other people. All of those experiences create energies that are taken through the door of death to become part of your existence as an eternal soul.

Each day, notice how much time that you spend on the superficial experiences, and how much on experiences of depth. Do not criticize yourself if you decide that you are out of balance. Simply make some changes so that your life experiences can be fuller and more satisfying.

As you become more and more enlightened on your pathway, you will feel an exceptional boundlessness and radiance in your daily life. You will know for certain that joy and beauty extend beyond the horizons of physical birth and death, into the magnificence of the eternal realm of your soul and the divine forces of life.

By opening your heart and mind to the extraordinary energies of love and beauty that come into you from your soul, you will be able to merge the human and the divine in the most beautiful way throughout your life. To guide yourself toward such a goal, say to yourself each day:

> "I begin my path of enlightenment by my willingness to be *human*—to live my human life honestly, courageously, and lovingly. Today, as I carry out my human activities, I will look for the beauty of the divine forces of life in myself, in other people, and in everything around me. *If I can find the magnificence of the divine in my moment to moment human experience, then I can find it everywhere.*"

Remind yourself each day: *You* are the master of your human consciousness. You can expand your consciousness through loving, diligent inner work, and through your growth in the outer world. That will lead you to live and express the true magnificence of your soul while you are in human form. If you do that day by day, then you will rejoice throughout this lifetime.

Your path of enlightenment will not only lead to your personal fulfillment in life, but you will also become the kind of person who brings goodness to the people around you. Your personal fulfillment, aligned with the goodness that you give to others, will lead to a *mastery* of life on earth. You will complete your own soul's purposes, and, at the same time, you will be a part of the unfoldment of the larger purposes for the evolution of human life. You will play an important role in the enlightenment of humanity on earth.

For more information about the work of Dr. Ron Scolastico, visit: www.ronscolastico.com; or call: 1-800-359-3771